T0339500

Business History

The evolution of business history offers some radical ways forward for a discipline which is rich in potential. This shortform book offers an expert overview of how the field has relevance for contemporary business studies as well as the social sciences more broadly, as well as practitioners interested in historical perspectives.

This book not only provides a comprehensive review of how the discipline of business history has evolved over the last century, but it also lays out an agenda for the next decade. Focusing specifically on the 'three pillars' of research, teaching and practical impact, the authors have outlined how while the first has flourished across many continents, the latter two are struggling to overcome significant challenges associated with how the discipline is perceived, especially in the social sciences. A solution is proposed that would involve academics working more closely with practitioners, thereby increasing the discipline's credibility across key stakeholders.

The work here presented provides a concise and easily digestible overview of the topic which will be of interest to scholars, researchers and advanced students focusing on the evolution of business history and its impact on the way the world conducts business today.

John F. Wilson is Professor of Business History at Newcastle Business School, Northumbria University, UK.

Ian G. Jones is a Senior Research Associate at Northumbria University, UK.

Steven Toms is Professor of Accounting at Leeds University Business School, University of Leeds, UK.

Anna Tilba is Associate Professor in Strategy and Governance at the Durham University Business School, University of Durham, UK.

Emily Buchnea is Senior Lecturer at Newcastle Business School, Northumbria University, UK.

Nicholas Wong is Vice Chancellor's Senior Research Fellow at Newcastle Business School, Northumbria University, UK.

State of the Art in Business Research
Series Editor: Geoffrey Wood

Recent advances in theory, methods and applied knowledge (alongside structural changes in the global economic ecosystem) have presented researchers with challenges in seeking to stay abreast of their fields and navigate new scholarly terrains.

State of the Art in Business Research presents shortform books which provide an expert map to guide readers through new and rapidly evolving areas of research. Each title will provide an overview of the area, a guide to the key literature and theories and time-saving summaries of how theory interacts with practice.

As a collection, these books provide a library of theoretical and conceptual insights, and exposure to novel research tools and applied knowledge, that aid and facilitate in defining the state of the art, as a foundation stone for a new generation of research.

Gossip, Organization and Work
A Research Overview
Kathryn Waddington

Remote Working
A Research Overview
Alan Felstead

Business History
A Research Overview
John F. Wilson, Ian G. Jones, Steven Toms, Anna Tilba, Emily Buchnea and Nicholas Wong

For more information about this series, please visit: www.routledge.com/State-of-the-Art-in-Business-Research/book-series/START

Business History
A Research Overview

John F. Wilson, Ian G. Jones,
Steven Toms, Anna Tilba,
Emily Buchnea and
Nicholas Wong

Routledge
Taylor & Francis Group

LONDON AND NEW YORK

First published 2022
by Routledge
4 Park Square, Milton Park, Abingdon, Oxon OX14 4RN

and by Routledge
605 Third Avenue, New York, NY 10158

Routledge is an imprint of the Taylor & Francis Group, an informa business

British Library Cataloguing-in-Publication Data
A catalogue record for this book is available from the British Library

Library of Congress Cataloging-in-Publication Data
Names: Wilson, J. F., author. | Jones, Ian G., 1987- author. | Toms, Steven, author.
Title: Business history : a research overview / John F. Wilson, Ian G. Jones, Steven Toms, Anna Tilba, Emily Buchnea and Nicholas Wong.
Description: 1 Edition. | New York, NY : Routledge, 2022. | Series: State of the art in business research | Includes bibliographical references and index.
Identifiers: LCCN 2021051836 (print) | LCCN 2021051837 (ebook) | ISBN 9781138326989 (hardback) | ISBN 9781032246628 (paperback) | ISBN 9780429449536 (ebook)
Subjects: LCSH: Business—History. | Business enterprises—History. | Industries—History. | Economic history. | Industrial management—History.
Classification: LCC HF352 .W535 2022 (print) | LCC HF352 (ebook) | DDC 382.09—dc23/eng/20211123
LC record available at https://lccn.loc.gov/2021051836
LC ebook record available at https://lccn.loc.gov/2021051837

ISBN: 978-1-138-32698-9 (hbk)
ISBN: 978-1-032-24662-8 (pbk)
ISBN: 978-0-429-44953-6 (ebk)

DOI: 10.4324/9780429449536

Typeset in Times New Roman
by codeMantra

Contents

Preface

The authors would like to thank Terry Clague of Routledge for both commissioning this book and his enduring patience while we struggled with personal and pandemic-related issues. It has been a great privilege to build on *The Routledge Companion to Business History*, especially as we were able to recruit three additional authors to complement the coverage we had already achieved in the original editorial team. This book is dedicated to all those business historians who have contributed to what is now a voluminous literature and especially to those who feature in the following pages. We hope that the book stimulates a wide debate about the future of a discipline which is relatively new to academia but which possesses terrific creativity and drive.

John Wilson, Ian Jones, Steven Toms, Anna Tilba,
Emily Buchnea and Nicholas Wong

Abbreviations

ABH	Association of Business Historians
BAC	Business Archives Council
BHC	Business History Conference
CBHA/ACHA	Canadian Business History Association–l'Association Canadienne pour l'Histoire des Affaires
EBHA	European Business History Association
GUG	Gesellschaft für Unternehmensgeschichte
MHRG	Management History Research Group
MOS	management and organizational studies
REF	(UK) Research Excellence Framework

1 Introduction

This new book builds on the core collection of ideas provided in the *Routledge Companion to Business History* (Wilson et al., 2016). Specifically, in further elaborating on the *Companion*'s multi-perspective approach, we aim both to explain the progress that business history as a discipline has made and assess how this can be sustained, focusing on what we regard as the three pillars of research, teaching and practical impact. A key issue in this respect will be assessing why business history has made considerable progress in terms of the research pillar yet failed to make much of an impact in the other two areas. Indeed, in spite of the increased tendency of business historians to find employment in business or management schools, the discipline has been marginalized, even ignored, due to a highly normative and functional approach to teaching business and management. Although Suddaby (2016; p. 47) has claimed that 'it is an exceptionally good time to be a business historian', emphasizing how leading management scholars have made strenuous efforts to assimilate business history into social science disciplines such as organization studies, strategy and international business, it certainly remains the case that there is very little evidence of business school curricula adapting to what has been happening in many management journals. Similarly, one would struggle to detect a business historian contributing to executive education as a historian, while in spite of encouragement from a former Governor of the Bank of England (Carney, 2020) policymakers rarely even consider the lessons to be learned from the past. Although the discipline continues to exhibit considerable vitality and vibrancy, attracting scholars from a variety of disciplines, it remains to be seen whether this has benefited business history research, teaching and practical impact.

In this book, we shall delve more deeply into these debates, elaborating further on one of the core aims of the *Companion*, namely, our desire to provide 'an introduction to, and overview of, current

DOI: 10.4324/9780429449536-1

scholarship in the expanding discipline of business history, using a structure that builds the research agenda and at the same time offering thematic perspectives on major business issues and problems'. Our focus on the three pillars of research, teaching and practical impact will also help to expose the clear view of 'a discipline that continues to evolve, and especially by both extending its coverage and building much stronger links with the social sciences' (Wilson et al., 2016; p. 8). By developing further this multi-perspective approach, we will be better able to establish the evolutionary path on which business history seems destined to tread and propose a route for the future.

Before moving on to assess how we intend to tackle these issues, it is essential to outline specifically what we regard as business history. In the *Companion*, it was claimed that 'business history is concerned with understanding how business organizations evolve, in their institutional, national and international contexts through managerial process, by engaging with a variety of source material'. This built on Wilson's (1995; p. 1) earlier definition of the discipline, which stated that:

> The main aim of business history is to study and explain the behaviour of the firm over long periods of time, and to place the conclusions in a broader framework composed of the markets and institutions in which that behaviour occurs.

Of course, the latter highlights the principal focus on both business organizations and the application of historical research methodologies, leading others to claim that it fails to capture a more recent interest in multiple other approaches and orientations. Nevertheless, we remain committed to the view that business history is at heart an empirically based discipline, with the important caveat that 'if business historians want to contribute to broader debates…it is essential to engage with a variety of methodologies' (Toms & Wilson, 2017; pp. 16–17). These points were earlier noted by Yacob (2009; pp. 302–303), who wrote that:

> Business history is an essential complementary analytical tool to provide insights into business-related topics that might otherwise be overlooked by other disciplines. Its evolutionary and historical perspectives help to broaden the study of diverse aspects of business systems, a contribution that is rarely fully acknowledged.

Álvaro-Moya and Donzé (2016; p. 124) also claimed that 'business history is a discipline at the crossroads between history and management science', highlighting the enormous potential in a more rigorous collaboration between these two areas of scholarly endeavour. *Above all, we regard business history as a window on key aspects of society and human activity, providing a rich, nuanced, empirically based understanding of how business interacts with and influences the world around it.* We are especially committed to applying what Andrews and Burke (2007) describe as the 'five Cs of historical thinking' of context, change over time, causality, complexity and contingency. At no stage will we argue that business history needs to be subsumed into, for example, the recently formed school of historical organization studies or, indeed, any other social science methodology; our aim is to outline the mutual benefits of cross-fertilization and ensure that business history continues to flourish as a discipline in its own right.

This bold statement will provide the book with a consistent thread, in that in charting both the way business history has evolved and its future prospects, we shall be concerned with how the three pillars of research, teaching and impact have been affected by its interaction with external influences. As we shall see in Chapter 2, which provides a 'history of business history', from its early days the discipline has been influenced by different disciplines, from (industrial) economics through to strategic decision-making, organization studies and international business. At the same time, one might add that despite what were at times serious flirtations with the social sciences, these dalliances have never proved decisive in moving business history away from its roots as a humanities subject. Moreover, while in research terms the discipline gathered significant momentum, especially from the 1970s, there was little spill-over into teaching and impact. This is perhaps best exemplified through an analysis of Chandler's contributions because there is little doubt that in the 1960s and 1970s his work was influencing all three pillars, providing business history with extensive opportunities to establish an unstoppable momentum. On the other hand, we shall see that this proved to be a false start for the discipline, especially once the many limitations of the Chandlerian model were highlighted.

The remainder of Chapter 2 will provide further illustrations of how in spite of this false start business history research continued to flourish, partially fuelled by the development of professional associations and the emergence of fresh journal outlets. This theme will be developed much further in Chapters 3 and 4, where it will be made clear that especially from the 1990s social scientists were attracted to the use of history, and business history specifically, as a means of enlivening their own disciplines. The proliferation of journal special issues has been especially noticeable, illustrating how prominent social scientists have succeeded in illustrating the possibilities in cross-fertilization and prompting Suddaby (2016; p. 47) to make the claim quoted earlier. At the same time, it is clear that of our three pillars, only research has benefited, rather than teaching and impact. This theme is further illustrated in Chapter 5, which assesses business history's links with the disciplines of international business and strategy.

Chapter 6 switches the emphasis to teaching business history, offering a detailed view of how the discipline can inveigle its way into business school curricula especially. The growing tendency of business historians to pursue careers in business schools has certainly created tensions for these scholars, in that while they are allowed to pursue their own research agendas, it is increasingly obvious that the pressures to publish in management, rather than history, journals are decisively altering their identity. At the same time, and especially in those institutions that espouse a belief in research-led/informed teaching, the acute paucity of business history modules or programmes poses an additional challenge, while rarely would one find those scholars participating in executive education as historians. This challenges the core competencies of a business historian, in that as Popp and Fellman (2020) have elaborated, their training is based on understanding historic context, processes of continuity and change and the construction of chronology, rather than theoretical analysis and conducting research into current and future developments. Specifically, this prompts questions associated with the value, function and purpose of business history in business schools, given that curricula fail to accommodate the discipline and the appeal to both students and practitioners (including policymakers) is allegedly limited.

It is into this debate that Chapter 7 ventures, outlining in provocative fashion how social science and business history journals are more concerned with the theoretical dimensions of their respective disciplines, rather than explaining how the research might influence the worlds of practice. In many ways, this reflects a wider debate relating to the intrinsic value of management education because on both sides of the Atlantic business schools have been heavily criticized for an inability to generate the kind of skillsets required in practice (Wilson, 1996). Chapter 4 will consequently outline how business history research can contribute to the development of a deeper understanding both of business per se and its place in society, focusing on specific examples of how this can be achieved.

In the concluding chapter, we shall draw together the various themes that have dominated the book and provide readers with a view of how business history can develop in the 2020s. Although one might expect some debate to arise from what we advocate, our view is that business history ought to stay true to its strengths as an empirically based discipline that has the potential to interact with the social sciences. We also certainly agree with Kipping et al. (2016; p. 19), who have noted that business history 'is in an inventive mood, bursting with multiple futures and paths forward', albeit with the important caveat that the discipline needs to assert its own identity, rather than be absorbed into the work of social scientists who regard empirical evidence as mere supporting data for their theoretical perspectives. Above all, we want business historians to realize the strengths of the discipline and continue to advance the research agenda in order to influence both teaching and impact, an aim that is not beyond the abilities of those scholars with the ambition and drive to make it happen.

There is clearly a range of challenging issues facing both business history as a discipline and business historians in general. In addition to what has just been noted, one can add other questions, such as the extent to which contiguous areas of study such as management history, accounting history and economic history influence the discipline. This aspect of the debate also begs another important question related to understanding what new themes are emerging, especially those related to corporate governance, ethics and sustainability. Crucially, it is important to understand who should be reading business history. Is it incumbent on business historians to widen the appeal of the discipline, not only to social scientists but also to business practitioners and policymakers? Is it sufficient merely to demand that business history is accorded the same level of respect as either social science disciplines or other forms of historical analysis? The future remains challenging; yet business historians have the ability and scope to make a greater contribution than offering longitudinal perspectives to current and future debates; it is our responsibility to make this happen.

2   A history of business history

In charting the evolution of this discipline, it is important to remember that we do so from a vantage point that can look back on a century of considerable growth in business history research; previously, economic history had been the prime focal point for those interested in studying firms, entrepreneurs and related matters. This chapter will be concerned with charting what can only be described as a transformational process, capturing how a specific discipline emerged out of a variety of influences. Of undoubted importance to this analysis will be the historical school of economics, given both its methodological approach and the impact these scholars had on the American pioneers of business history. This will provide an opportunity to explain why Harvard Business School became the first higher education institution to establish a chair in business history as well as how A.D. Chandler would emerge as the doyen of business historians in the 1960s. Given Chandler's influence on the discipline for at least thirty years, it will also be important to provide an analysis of his various contributions in order to understand the nature of his influence and its wider impact on research, teaching and practitioners. Controversially, we shall assess whether Chandler was a false start for business history because such was the mounting criticisms of his work by the 1980s and 1990s that the discipline was bereft of an anchor-point.

Having delved into this aspect of the evolutionary story, it will be essential to chart parallel developments in other countries. This exercise will demonstrate in graphic form how different social science disciplines influenced the approach to business history, albeit in fragmented and ephemeral ways. One might describe these as a series of flirtations, starting with economics and moving on to strategic decision-making, international business and, most recently, organization studies. As most economic history departments were either closing or being severely rationalized from the 1990s, and an increasing proportion of

DOI: 10.4324/9780429449536-2

business historians were also finding more secure employment in business or management schools, these flirtations reflected significant changes across academia that radically influenced the way business history was perceived. At the same time, however, and emphasizing a key theme of the chapter, business historians struggled to find an identity that was both respected and aligned to contiguous disciplines, setting up the challenge that must be addressed in the 2020s.

2.1 Early stages

One of the more fascinating aspects of how business history has evolved over the last 120 years is the extent to which multiple influences would appear to have helped fashion the discipline, providing a kaleidoscopic image that is at times difficult to interpret. Figure 2.1 offers a simple chronology outlining what we regard as the key approaches and disciplines that have influenced the nature and orientation of business history at different points over the last 130 years. Given this eclectic range of influences, it is perhaps no surprise to many that for decades business history has struggled to be identified as a discipline in its own right, not least because in many countries it was regarded as merely a sub-discipline of economic history. Crucially, it is clear that three of the first four rows have been continuous influences on the nature of business history, and especially 'Corporate History', because a significant proportion of the research has been focused on the firm. At the same time, as Kipping et al. (2016; p. 21) explain, 'the roots of modern histories of business lay in the deeper past, and particularly in the emergence of the "historical school of economics" in Germany and the UK'. This claim has been supported by other prominent academics, including Wadhwani and Lubinski (2017) and Jones and Friedman (2017), highlighting how the historical school of economics, or what is today known as industrial economics (Devine et al., 1985), proved to be highly influential. There are three key dimensions of the discipline which appeal to business historians: it employs an inductive methodology that focused on real-time events, rather than the abstractions of deductive classical economics; these empirical investigations focused on the ways in which institutional frameworks and human behaviour interact and historical economists believed 'in the practical value of historical knowledge for decision making' (Kipping et al., 2016; pp. 21–22). Crucially, the first Dean of Harvard Business School, E.F. Gray, was educated by the leading German historical economist, Gustav von Schmoller, resulting in that institution developing the case-study approach to management education. Gray's successor, W.B.

	1880	1920	...	1960	1980	2004	2020
Economics ^							→
Economic History							→
Entrepreneurial Hist.							→
Corporate History							→
Chandler				→			
Comparative Studies							→
'Historic Turn'							→
'New' Business History							→
Historical Org Studies							▷
Memory Studies							→

Figure 2.1 Key influences on Business History, 1880–2020.
^ 'Economics' is here defined as the Historical School of Economics, or as it has come to be known, Industrial Economics.

Donham, was also responsible for the introduction of business history into the HBS curriculum, supporting the formation of a Business Historical Society (1925) and approving a business history course (1927). It was also in 1927 that the Isidor Strauss Chair in Business History was first endowed, by the owners of Macy's department store, establishing a lineage of highly distinguished scholars that continues to this day (Kipping et al., 2016; p. 22).

As the United States was alone in developing university-based management education until much later in the twentieth century (Wilson, 1995), the seedbed for a similar development of business history was slow to evolve in the United Kingdom and Europe. Instead, the historical school of economics was responsible in the United Kingdom for the emergence of economic history as a discipline in its own right during the 1920s, with Japan imitating this movement at the same time (Kipping et al., 2016; pp. 23–24). This is a vital insight into the evolutionary process, albeit with a clear understanding that while by the 1950s what had increasingly come to be named industrial economics was more concerned with economic theorizing, especially of business behaviour, economic history until the 1970s remained entirely empirical in orientation and output. This bifurcation occurred in spite of the significant achievements of a series of British industrial economists, from W. Ashley (1914) and R.L. Hall and C.J. Hitch (1939) through to the highly innovative 1950s work of P.W.S. Andrews (the founding editor of the *Journal of Industrial Economics*) on industrial analysis and Edith Penrose (1959) on the theory of the growth of the firm. The key issue here is the inductive methodology employed by industrial economists, a methodology which would not have been alien to many economic historians. Penrose's highly innovative approach is especially noticeable, in that it pre-empted later work on dynamic capabilities by Teece et al. (1997) in focusing on the firm as 'a collection of productive resources the disposal of which between different uses and over time is determined by administrative decision' (Penrose, 1959; p. 24). As this original insight focused attention directly on a firm's management as its principal determinant of the rate of growth, Penrose could well have provided both a methodological and theoretical basis for the small group of business historians that emerged in the United States and the United Kingdom between the 1920s and 1960s. It is clear, however, that this opportunity has never been seized by business historians, highlighting a theme to which we shall return when assessing Pettigrew's later work on strategic change (1985).

As we noted earlier, business history was slow to emerge in the United Kingdom, principally because of the paucity of university-level management education, while economic history proved to be the chosen path for those who preferred longitudinal studies of industry and firms. Of significance, however, was the formation in 1934 of the Business Archives Council (BAC), which benefitted from building up a membership base of businesses and businesspeople, libraries and other institutions as well as individual archivists, records managers, businesspeople and historians (Anson, 2010). Although the BAC has consistently struggled against the widespread corporate tendency to shred invaluable records, its missionary work has proved successful in ensuring that business people recognize the value in preservation. The publication of a journal (*Business Archives*) from 1965 also provided opportunities for a genuine interchange between the various stakeholders, while later the BAC built close links with the professional business history associations that emerged from the 1990s as a further means of pursuing its mission to save and value business archives.

Regardless of the BAC's sterling work, however, business history as a discipline continued to be regarded as a sub-field of economic history. The outputs of successive professors of economic history at the University of Manchester demonstrates this point clearly because although T.S. Ashton, W. Chaloner and A.E. Musson provided detailed studies of leading engineering firms that acted as a major influence on the activities of the next generation of business historians, they resolutely remained economic historians. Ironically, though, it was an Economic and Social History department that sparked the first robust developments in British business history when a group of academics at the University of Liverpool led by F.E. Hyde and Sheilagh Marriner established *Business History*. This coincided with a growing interest amongst large-scale firms in commissioning established economic historians to write detailed histories, starting with Unilever (Wilson, 1954) and later including Courtaulds (Coleman, 1969), W.D. & H.O. Wills (Alford, 1973) and Pilkington's (Barker, 1976). Other universities also contained scholars who started to show a nascent interest, especially Glasgow, which in 1970 established the first UK post dedicated to business history. The inaugural occupant was Tony Slaven, who later became Britain's first professor of business history and in 1987 established the Centre for Business History in Scotland, attracting a substantial private donation that has sustained this body as a major contributor to the discipline's development. It is also notable that Slaven was instrumental in the formation of the Association of Business Historians (1990), using his Centre's private benefaction to bring a critical mass of academics together to provide a focus for the discipline. There were also significant contiguous developments in Lancaster, Manchester and Reading, while as we shall see later in 1978 the London School of Economics established the pioneering Business History Unit, headed by the highly influential Leslie Hannah (Jones & Sluyterman, 2003). Interestingly, though, in none of the rapidly growing British business schools did business history feature specifically in either staff recruitment or their programmes, establishing a tradition that persists into the 2020s. This point is well illustrated by the disappointing response to the Social Science Research Council's 1981 offer of funding for appointments to business history posts because only London Business School responded by hiring one person. Clearly, the opportunities for business historians were few and far between.

2.2 The impact of A.D. Chandler, jnr

Even though the historical school of economics was arguably more influential in the United States, and Harvard had clearly succeeded in establishing business history as a topic of interest for both research and teaching, one should not exaggerate the pace of development because by the 1950s the latter was still regarded as a marginal subject. Of course, Gras had firmly established the case study as a principal pedagogic dimension of HBS's programmes, an approach that prevails today. On the other hand, his insistence that business history was 'primarily the study of the administration of business units of the past' (Gras & Larson, 1939; p. 3) severely limited its appeal to both historians and social scientists. To a certain extent, the discipline retains a reputation for adopting this narrow scope because as Figure 2.1 reveals corporate history has been a continuous activity over the last hundred years, focusing on an internalized study of a firm's organization that failed to excite interest outside a narrow group that revolved around Gras' network.

Having highlighted the severe limitations of the approach that Gras and his followers chose, it is also vital to stress that in 1948 HBS established a Research Center in Entrepreneurial History, following the work of Arthur Cole, a professor of business economics who had been tutored by E.F. Gay. Supported by a multidisciplinary team of scholars, this activity demonstrates how even within HBS there were deep divisions that reflected different methodological approaches to the study of business (Jones & Friedman, 2017). Similarly, rather than the case-study methodology espoused by Harvard, many other US business schools developed their own pedagogy that was more closely linked to economics and quantitative analysis, further limiting HBS's impact. Even though what in 1953 was converted into the *Business History Review* had been started in 1938, the discipline was struggling to break into the mainstream of US academia, whether that be management studies or historical research. Regardless of these differences, by 1954 a Business History Conference (BHC) had been formed as a national, and later international, forum for those academics who were interested in the subject. As we shall see later, although the BHC struggled to match the much larger professional associations that dominated the American academic scene, once it moved its administrative base to the Hagley Museum and Library after its 1987 conference, it became a major influence on the discipline. Indeed, the BHC has become a genuinely international association, not only through its membership but also by arranging joint conferences with British and European associations, highlighting the extensive possibilities in this kind of interaction.

All this, however, lay in the future because by the early 1960s business history had yet to make a significant impact on academia. The publication in 1962 of *Strategy and Structure* by Alfred D. Chandler would decisively alter that image. Chandler had realized the limitations of the Harvard approach to business history, persuading him to write a book that would compare organizational structures and explore strategic processes (Chandler, 1978). By pursing this comparative mode, Chandler hoped to contribute to a better understanding of how large companies evolved and operated, rather than merely providing the specifics of how a particular company worked. He had already produced a study of the fifty largest US industrial companies (Chandler, 1956), but in *Strategy and Structure*, Chandler focused on just four companies – Du Pont, General Motors, Standard Oil (New Jersey) and Sears, Roebuck. One of his principal conclusions was that 'different organizational forms result from different types of growth' (1962; p. 12), namely, that strategy determines structure. For the purposes of this argument, Chandler defined strategy as 'the determination of the basic long-term goals and objectives of an enterprise, and the adoption of courses of action and allocation of resources necessary for carrying out these goals', noting that strategic changes are made 'in response to the opportunities and needs created by changing populations and changing national income and by technological innovation'. Structure was defined as 'the design of organization through which the enterprise is administered', with structural changes often lagging behind strategic change until existing administrative structures become too inefficient to manage the organization's growth. Various reasons were given for executives' failure to respond and adapt their organization's structure, such as either ignorance of the new administrative needs of the organization's structure or because structural reorganization could threaten their position, power or 'psychological security'.

Chandler's work in *Strategy and Structure* was regarded as a major step forward in developing a theoretical model for organizational change and development. Specifically, in terms of our three pillars, the book proved to be highly influential, in that: it reinforced and extended the case study mode of teaching; Chandler's ideas later helped to fashion fresh insights into the theory of the firm and in terms of impact, it was claimed that management consultants at McKinsey & Co adopted the book as essential reading. With specific regard to theoretical contributions, even though Chandler never claimed to be anything but a business historian, he undoubtedly contributed to other disciplines. For example, Whittington (2008; p. 267) noted that 'Chandler was a fundamental influence on the shape of the strategic management discipline', and especially the study of strategy as practice. There is also no doubt that Chandler helped indirectly to fashion the early development of the resource-based view (RBV) of the firm in the 1980s, especially the work of Rumelt, Barney and Wernerfelt (Whittington, 2008; p. 272). The Nobel Economics Prize winner O.E. Williamson (1985) also credited Chandler with making a contribution to the development of transaction cost economics because he applied Chandlerian concepts in explaining different governance structures as a means of overcoming market challenges. Similarly, although he later went on to present an extensive critique of Chandler's work (Fligstein, 2008), as a sociologist Fligstein (2008a; p. 249) felt that *Strategy and Structure* 'pioneered the study of real corporations undergoing real transformation'. Indeed, it is difficult to think of another business history text that has had such a pervasive impact on social science thinking and, in particular, on a range of novel developments that would help to fashion whole new fields of research.

Another dimension of this book was the emphasis Chandler placed on the multidivisional form (M-form) of organization, arguing that the extent to which American corporations adopted this model to accommodate their increasingly extensive diversification strategies was another reason why they proved to be so dynamic and competitive. As Amatori and Colli (2007) have demonstrated, this was one of the principal reasons why economists such as Williamson and Teece found reading Chandler so rewarding. Of course, many have since challenged Chandler's simplistic view on the relationship between diversification strategies and organizational responses, not least because in some of the cases Chandler used management experienced severe difficulties in implementing the M-form (Freeland, 1993). As we shall also note later, other economies achieved considerable success without replicating the M-form. Nevertheless, because in the 1960s the US economy was increasingly regarded as the template for others to imitate if they are going to harness the extensive benefits of rapid technological progress combined with increased standards of living across the industrialized world, academics from four European countries (Germany, France, Italy and the United Kingdom) were recruited by HBS into what was labelled 'The Harvard Project' (Amatori & Colli, 2007). Focusing on the period 1950–1970, this resulted in several publications which contributed extensively to a deeper understanding of the relationship between strategy and structure. Of particular note were the studies by Channon (1973) on British business, Pavan (1977, cited in Amatori & Colli, 2007) on the Italian case, while Dyas and Thanheiser (1974) provided a comparative study of France and West Germany. At the same time, it is essential to note that none of these authors would have regarded themselves as business historians; rather, they were using longitudinal studies of business systems to provide deeper insights into the interaction between strategy and structure. This work also later stimulated the innovative work of Whittington and Mayer (2000), which extended Channon's analysis of British business's extensive adoption of the M-form from the 1960s, opening up new debates for business historians in relation to strategic management.

In generating this wave of publications, Chandler had established himself as the leading business historian of his time (McCraw, 1997). In an intellectual sense, one might argue that his greatest legacy was the debates he stimulated as business historians especially responded to both the methodology he employed and the assumptions relating to the influence on corporate evolution of both internal and external factors. For example, Alford (1977; p. 117) noted that Chandler's preoccupation with the highest levels of management meant that 'diffused entrepreneurship' lower down the hierarchy was ignored. These insights challenged business historians to analyse in greater detail the hierarchical diagrams in which Chandler put such great store. Moreover, it questions whether in practice structure determines strategy, rather than the other way round, with functional departments potentially having a much greater effect on strategy than Chandler anticipated, either through influencing the information that reaches executives about markets and technological trends or by attempting to adopt policies that protected their own interests. Additionally, Chandler's analysis has been criticized for downplaying the strength of external factors more generally, such as the role of government in markets, or the socio-cultural environment in which the organization operates. It is only fair to note, however, that Chandler (1962; p. 150) regarded the findings presented in *Strategy and Structure* as a basis for further work on the development of business administration in the United States. Chandler's next book, *The Visible Hand* (1977), would build on these findings and look to answer some of these criticisms.

Prior to the publication of *The Visible Hand*, however, in responding to an invitation from Hannah in 1975 to contribute to what was labelled a 'Management History Conference' at the London School of Economics (Kennedy & Payne, 1976), it was apparent by the early 1970s that Chandler was also working on a comparative study of the United Kingdom and the United States. Anticipating his later work and building on the analysis conducted by Channon (1973), Chandler highlighted the extent to which business practices were converging in the United States and the United Kingdom, especially if one focused on the interactions between diversification strategies and the adoption of an M-form structure. Linking back to an earlier piece written by Daems (Chandler & Daems, 1974), he also reiterated his views on the three key stages through which both individual businesses and national business systems have passed, providing the terms *Personal*, *Entrepreneurial* and *Managerial* to define these stages. While others (Wilson & Thomson, 2006; Quail, 2000) have adapted this typology to provide a more nuanced understanding of British business evolution, Chandler was once again offering an original perspective to comprehend the staging process. With specific regard to the United Kingdom, he also argued that the persistence of family owner-management had restricted organizational evolution in the United Kingdom (Chandler, 1976), anticipating a debate that would flare up in the 1990s. Indeed, the 1975 conference papers by Alford (1976) and Hannah (1976) especially demonstrated some of the shortcomings of Chandler's claims about the alleged backward nature of British business organization, material the American chose to ignore when he developed a later monograph.

Apart from contending Chandler's claims about the relative weakness of *Personal Capitalism*, British business historians have also challenged the staging process. For example, in developing a conceptual framework based on 'the notion that business is always in transition, strategically and structurally, governed by interactions of scale and scope economy exploitation and accountability of external stakeholders', Toms and Wilson (2003; p. 1) provide compelling arguments against using the 'stages' approach to explain business evolution. Crucially, this conceptual framework sets out a substantial agenda for research into business evolution, undermining the simplistic labels offered by Chandler that prove to be atheoretical and even ahistorical. As we shall also see towards the end of this section, the framework resonates with the recent surge in interest in corporate governance issues, reflecting once again how business historians were increasingly moving away from the Chandlerian preoccupation with internal perspectives of the firm.

Returning to *The Visible Hand*, Chandler argued that between the 1880s and 1920s a salaried management class in the United States 'took the place of the market mechanisms in coordinating many of the activities of the economy and allocating its resources' (Chandler, 1977; p. 1). When combined with the benefits arising from a 'Second Industrial Revolution', resulting in the emergence of new industries such as electrical engineering, automobiles and pharmaceuticals, professional managers took on the role of co-ordinating resources throughout existing production and design processes and allocating personnel and funds in preparation for future production and distribution. Indeed, the emergence of the M-form of organization was based on the reinforcement of managerial power, rather than achieving economies of scale and scope (Dobbin, 1994; Freeland, 1993; Fligstein, 2008). The 'visible hand' of management consequently showed itself to be more efficient in distributing resources than the 'invisible hand' of the market, conferring a competitive advantage on businesses that linked the administration of production and distribution. Responding to those who had earlier criticized Chandler for ignoring the role of external factors, he argued that although factors such as the role of the state had been important, the development of a salaried managerial class was an internalization of responsibilities that had previously been externalized in markets. As the managerial class increased its level of influence within businesses and across society, they were able to replace ownership in directing the strategy and structure of these businesses because of their control over internalized processes, thereby generating higher profits and shaping the markets in which they operated.

Chandler followed up *The Visible Hand* with a third monograph, *Scale and Scope* (1990). As we noted earlier, Chandler had been working on a US-UK comparative study since the 1970s, offering contentious views at the LSE's 1975 Management History Conference on both the staging of business evolution and the reasons why British business had been slow to move towards the allegedly more robust American model (Chandler, 1976). This thesis was further developed and extended in *Scale and Scope* by comparing the top 200 industrial companies in the United States, Britain and Germany between 1880 and 1950. The core point was the claim that the US style of managerial capitalism was superior and should be the path other industrial economies ought to follow. What this meant in practice was the proposition that corporate success required investment in what can be categorized as 'three M's': manufacturing facilities that were large enough to take advantage of economies of scale and scope; marketing and distribution to keep pace with increased production and management capable of administering these firms. Organizations that made these investments were able to dominate their markets, competing for more by improving their products, production processes, marketing, purchasing, labour relations or moving into new sectors and markets more quickly and effectively than their competitors (Chandler, 1990; p. 8).

While many regarded these core ideas in *Scale and Scope* as valuable insights into the rapid growth of American corporations, the comparisons with German and British businesses were much more controversial. Although Chandler argued that the German case came close to the US ideal, albeit operating more co-operatively than in the United States, British businesses were heavily criticized for sticking to *personal capitalism* as the principal mode of organization. In particular, Chandler (1990; pp. 235–237, 389–398, 587–590) argued that the failure to invest in the 'three M's' was attributable to an extensive commitment to family control and ownership, a mode of organization that allegedly limited the availability of funds for investment because the bulk of corporate profit was paid in dividends to the owners. Crucially, Chandler felt that the British failure to compete internationally in Second Industrial Revolution sectors such as electrical engineering, automobiles and pharmaceuticals was attributable to the continued allegiance to *personal capitalism*, leaving the markets open for German and US firms to dominate.

Not surprisingly, *Scale and Scope* was met with much stronger criticism than his earlier works, significantly enlivening business history journals and conferences for many years. As Scranton (1991; p. 1103) noted in a scathing critique: 'The usual Chandler bracketings apply. Labour, culture, state policies, and all industrial activity outside the Top 200 are set aside as secondary or irrelevant'. Scranton went on to accuse Chandler of 'organizational determinism', in that *Scale and Scope* failed to accommodate the link between the role external factors play in determining both the strategies and structures adopted by firms. This highlights how Chandler ignored the work of another HBS professor, Michael Porter, who was at the time the *doyen* of strategy thinkers. Porter (1990; p. 786) was especially keen to emphasize how 'the environment surrounding firms...influences the creation of strategy, skills, organizational arrangements, and success in particular fields'. Moreover, Chandler's assumption that the US system of managerial capitalism was superior to others is an unfounded assertion that creates fundamental problems from the outset, ignoring the economic success enjoyed by other countries with different organizational structures. For example, during Japan's 'Economic Miracle' years between 1950 and the late 1980s, Japanese business was structured differently to the American model (Fruin, 1992). Indeed, although Fruin was commissioned by Chandler to research Japanese business for *Scale and Scope*, once it was apparent that the case did not fit with the core thesis, this work was side-lined. Crucially, such were the huge changes within American business at the time of the book's publication that it was inevitable Chandler's assertions about the superiority of managerial capitalism would be challenged. As Langlois (2004, p. 356) noted: 'What to do with a triumphalist history of something that is no longer triumphant?' This also relates to the point that Chandler's approach approximated to what is known as 'Whig history', namely, treating the time of writing as the final point of history, a wholly dangerous assumption for any historian (Lamoreaux et al., 2003, 2004).

It is consequently clear that *Scale and Scope* would never attain the critical heights achieved by Chandler's previous monographs. Indeed, the cavalcade of destructive criticism continued over the following twenty years, with Fligstein (2008) and Galambos (2010) amongst the most prominent of those who sought to qualify and contradict Chandler's claims. Above all, when we turn our attention specifically to his critique of *personal capitalism*, it is equally apparent that *Scale and Scope* was based on false assumptions. First, no quantitative evidence was produced to link *personal capitalism* with Britain's relatively poor economic performance, while the many counter examples of successful family owned businesses and developments in sectors outside of manufacturing were ignored. For example, while Chandler claims that Rio Tinto, a British owned mining firm, was a failure compared to various US mining companies, Hannah (2009) has demonstrated that Rio Tinto continued to be a global leader whilst the US firms had faded into obscurity. As Hannah asks, if such 'long-run outcomes are to be described as a "British failure" … it would be interesting to know precisely how Chandler would identify a twentieth-century success' (Hannah, 2009; p. 21).

Having noted these criticisms, however, it is nevertheless important to summarize Chandler's overall contribution to the development of business history. In the first place, as we noted earlier, *Strategy and Structure* provided a significant stimulus to each of our three pillars. In spite of the widespread condemnation of *Scale and Scope*, Chandler had also established a dominant narrative in the business history literature through his analysis of the rise of the large managerial corporation and the reasons for its success, particularly in the context of the institutional structures of the US economy up to 1980. Subsequent contributions can be broken down into three groups: first, those that build upon Chandler's model incrementally; second, those that recognize the key features but modify them in a significant fashion and third, those that set out competing and critical perspectives. By considering each of these, in turn, we can re-evaluate Chandler's contribution and the post-Chandler historiography.

Teece (1993) exemplified the incremental approach, namely, that business organizations are not shaped by markets, stressing that business organizations shape markets. As Chandler had shown, large firm behaviour is based on their specific internal characteristics, rather than oligopolistic market structures. Chandler claimed that contrasting governance explained the success of these large American firms, as distinct from their British counterparts; American managerial capitalism prioritized long-term objectives, whereas in Britain closely controlled businesses preferred to generate cash flows for their owner-managers. While this thesis is appealing, as it promotes a historical perspective on the co-evolution of firms and markets, on the other hand, it is also time-limited, as it explains the emergence and dominance of the US corporate model, which was already unravelling by the 1980s. Subsequent research has also offered explanations for the demise of the corporate conglomerate in the restructuring waves from the 1980s. For example, Lamoreaux et al. (2003) extended Chandler's model to explain the decline of the large corporation after 1980, facilitating the addition of new dimensions to Chandler's model and accommodating processes of accountability to capital markets and the suppliers of capital (Toms & Wilson, 2003). This alternative perspective complements external economies of scale and scope by theorizing the relationship between investments in competitive advantage assets and associated financial requirements. An extension of this approach was used to contrast British and US business history since 1945 (Toms & Wright, 2005a), demonstrating how the dominance of scale economies and financial constraints explains the apparent superiority of the Chanderian US corporate model up to 1980. Subsequently, besides internal economies of scale and scope, the possibility of conglomerate discount and similar diseconomies as well as external economies of scale and scope and network effects can be added. Evidence shows that these have become more prominent as determinants of corporate strategy and structure since 1980 (Toms & Wright, 2002, 2005b).

These new perspectives adapted the RBV of the firm, a theoretical perspective Chandler had influenced in the 1980s, especially the work of Rumelt, Barney and Wernerfelt (Whittington, 2008; p. 272). For Chandler, managers create the possibility of mass production as pragmatic problem solvers rather than bounded rationalists or opportunists (Fligstein, 2008; p. 244). First movers, achieving competitive advantage by making investments in production, distribution and administrative capacity, typically have advantages in embedding organizational learning and access to cheaper capital although unique isolating mechanisms cannot be necessarily achieved purely through investment in organizational processes (Toms & Wilson, 2012).

Examples of alternatives to the Chandler model include those that focus on external demand conditions. For example, Langlois and Robertson (1995) argue that the requirement for differentiated and individualized products undermined advantages associated with internal economies of scale. The labour process perspective offers a further alternative view of Chandler's claims, with Lazonick (2002) emphasizing the historical transformation of the labour process and the segmentation between managers and shop-floor workers as a barrier to organizational learning. Building on Chandler's model, he argues that investment in labour and new labour processes increased productivity but created additional fixed costs. However, only firms making such investments could achieve competitive advantage. Commitment to fixed cost investment also impacts the firm's ability to access finance, a point missing from Chandler's model (Lazonick, 2010, 2015). Toms (2010) has also provided a resource-based theorization of the relationship between fixed cost investment and the cost of finance, highlighting how the incorporation of economics into the analysis would have improved Chandler's approach.

Although seemingly critical, all of the contributions reviewed so far leave the main variables of Chandler's model intact. More strident critics, by contrast, offer alternative theorizations, which, in turn, frequently leads to empirical challenges. Whereas Chandler highlights the positive outcomes of managerial endeavour, he does not characterize management as a social class. Constituted thus, powerful executives could exercise their dominance through power networks and coalition building. Consequently, through lobbying and influence, they collude with elements of the state and state institutions, thereby reinforcing their market dominance (Roy, 1999; Prechel, 2000). Such accounts contrast sharply with Chandler's managers as innovators, potentially casting them instead as rent-seekers through regulatory capture.

Hoskin and Macve (1994) also focus on power and power dynamics, arguing that modern management cannot occur without controlling subordinate individuals within the organization, a process that is achieved through accounting. Adopting a Foucauldian perspective, they locate the genesis of modern management and associated management accounting techniques at West Point military academy and the application of control techniques through accounting at Springfield Armory in the 1840s. In doing so, they point out the limitations of Chandler's analysis (1977) of administrative efficiency at Springfield under an earlier management team led by Roswell Lee. As a critique of Chandler, this debate is unresolved because as Toms and Fleischman (2015) have subsequently noted through the provision of fresh empirical evidence that the Armory was anything but efficient in the 1840s and that the Hoskin and Macve account masked a plethora of corrupt managerial practices and inefficiencies.

Another area of unresolved debate is the RBV, which, as noted earlier, was constructed in part on Chandler's work. Criticisms of the RBV might consequently be applied in a similar vein to Chandler. For example, the empirical testability of the RBV has been called into question because it does not specify the process whereby firms generate profits (Bromiley & Fleming, 2002; pp. 325–326). Financial returns cannot be attributed to specific resources, while resource rents and their valuation do not accommodate risk, which could arise either between agents within the firm or between firm agents and the market (Toms, 2010). Insofar as the RBV is a theory of surplus, it is a theory of rents, not a theory of profit, further questioning Chandler's claims that the American model of managerial capitalism necessarily generated real competitive advantage. Furthermore, rent and rent-seeking by large industrial corporations open a further critique of Chandler's

model. Managerial hierarchy, lauded by Chandler as a source of innovation, nonetheless had the effect of crowding out entrepreneurship.
Toms et al. (2015) note that the dominance of the Chandlerian firm in
the 1950s and 1960s coincided with the 'death of the entrepreneur' and
that the development of the market for corporate control since 1980
has led to the rebirth of the entrepreneur, albeit not always applied
to productive purposes and, to some extent, implicated in the over-
dominance of financial innovation and financial services (Toms, 2018).

In a similar vein, historians seeking explanations for British economic decline since the late nineteenth century have invoked Chandler's account more systematically than any other (Hannah, 1999).
Critics of 'declinism' have pointed out that just as Chandler's story no
longer fits American enterprise since the 1980s, neither has it ever been
a particularly accurate description of British business history. This is
clear from subsequent evidence on economic performance, investment
in R&D and bank-industry relations (Edgerton, 1997). Hannah (1999)
offers an appealing critique that belies Chandler's explanation, noting
that as British economic performance has declined, there has not been
a similar decline in the influence of large firms. Indeed, large firms
have increased their dominance, such that by the 1990s Britain had
the highest levels of industrial concentration of any major economy
(Hannah, 1983). In contrast, while medium and smaller enterprises
have driven success in manufacturing in the United States and Germany, Hannah (1999) also suggests a revival of entrepreneurialism and
a boost in productivity coming from the smaller firm sector in Britain
after 1980.

Counterposing managerialism with entrepreneurship, the large
firm with the small firm, hints at further theoretical contrasts. Rowlinson et al. (2007) juxtapose Chandler's managerial narrative with
equally plausible 'anti-managerial' accounts. They first characterize
anti-managerialism as 'mainstream' and traceable to Berle and Means
(1932) and the subsequent development of agency-based models. Here,
the firm is nothing more than a nexus of contracts, and efficient capital
markets develop mechanisms to punish managerial inefficiency and
undermine managerial empire-building (Jensen, 1993). Alternatively,
Rowlinson et al. (2007) also identify a radical anti-managerialist account in which corporations, and their managers, were restrained according to the interests of a capitalist class, which, it might be argued,
offers an alternative explanation of the temporary dominance of large
corporations in the United States. While the decades 1950–1980 experienced a suppression of finance, thereby facilitating the growth of
the large industrial corporation, financial liberalization since 1980 has

undermined its dominance and reinforced banking and finance capital, not just in the United States but across the globe.

In summary, there are several reasons why business historians have moved beyond the Chandler model in recent decades. First, the Chandlerian firm was a temporary phenomenon, and its global success was attributable to the coincidence of favourable structural conditions in the United States between the 1950s and 1980s. Second, the prism of critical accounts reviewed above suggests that the Chandler model does not translate well in international contexts. Third, the managerial class was too hybrid and the structures of accountability were too variable, limiting its ability to choose a consistently rational path to competitive advantage, as opposed to the rent-seeking that comes with power, information asymmetry and monopoly. Finally, if we factor in the literature that adapts and develops the Chandler model, there are numerous gaps in the analysis and evidence, perhaps too numerous, leading business historians to seek alternative explanations of business evolution and competitive advantage. Nevertheless, Chandler not only inspired the discipline of strategic management but also provides present-day strategists with an alternative to the dominant quantitative model through re-engagement with business history. This highlights how business history can be a potential generator of new theory. Such potential can be enhanced through engagement with the broader social sciences, a point we shall develop further in later chapters.

2.3 Business history ex-Chandler

Having outlined the contributions Chandler made to the development of business history, as well as the wide range of critiques generated from other business historians and social scientists, it is important to note that many other approaches to the study of business history were being advocated by scholars in different parts of the world. Indeed, it would be grossly misleading to claim that the Chandlerian approach was universally followed by all business historians; even though there were enthusiastic supporters of the model, many others devoted considerable intellectual capital to the elaboration of alternative approaches. This re-emphasizes a point made earlier about the influences on business history (see Figure 2.1) because those scholars who came from either an economics/economic history background or the wider social sciences had been developing their own models. Although this is not the place for a compendious survey of every model that emerged in the late twentieth century, reviewing some of the more notable will highlight the diversity of approach that has come to characterize business history over the last fifty years. Crucially, a critical mass of business historians had by the 1990s emerged in the United States, Europe and Japan, as reflected in the emergence of new professional associations such as the BHC, ABH and EBHA which held dynamic and increasingly well-populated conferences and workshops that drew together scholars with both general and specific interests in the evolution of business as well as a search to understand its place in, and impact on, society. Similarly, some social scientists were utilizing business history in the development of theoretical models, pre-empting what would later become a significant influence on the discipline as it moved increasingly towards self-dependence. At the same time, it is noticeable that the inductive methodology preferred by industrial economists was largely neglected by business historians, a trend that was arguably a fundamental reason why the discipline failed to develop its own methodology.

Although it is always invidious to single out specific individuals for their role in developing business history, and national biases can limit broader perspectives, it is nevertheless fair to note that Leslie Hannah was responsible for significantly enhancing the discipline's reputation and impact from the 1970s. Not only was he made the first Director of LSE's Business History Unit (BHU) in 1977, from where other leading business historians emerged, but also Hannah's publications made a significant impact in providing a much-improved understanding of British, and later American, business evolution. In his inaugural lecture as the LSE's first professor of business history, Hannah was scathing in his criticism of the discipline's apparent preoccupation with single-case company histories, describing them as at best 'a triumph of narrative skill, honest to the facts of the individual case', at their worst 'narrow, insular, and antiquarian' (Hannah, 1983; p. 166). This is an issue later assessed by scholars such as Rowlinson and Procter (1999) and Rowlinson and Delahaye (2009), who castigated business historians for focusing largely on founder-centred narratives that failed to accommodate the much wider range of factors influencing business evolution. Hannah (1983; p. 167) was above all concerned that business history had developed in Britain in isolation from business schools, mainstream history, economics and the social sciences generally, setting up the expectation that the discipline ought to 'throw some light overlap quite naturally with questions to which industrial economists or industrial sociologists address themselves'. This links back to what was noted earlier about the potential impact that the industrial economist's inductive methodology could have had on a discipline that continued to be dominated by corporate history. In taking over the editorship of *Business History*, Hannah would also seize the opportunity to influence the nascent discipline at a decisive juncture, while the BHU succeeded in generating a plethora of high-quality academics who later went on to make a significant impact on business history (Foreman-Peck et al., 2019). Most notable of these were Geoffrey Jones, who would later become the Isidor Strauss Professor of Business History at Harvard as a result of his innovative work on international business, while David Jeremy contributed extensively as editor of the six-volume *Dictionary of Business Biography*.

Apart from the leadership that Hannah provided from the well-endowed BHU, he also generated a constant stream of highly influential books and articles (Foreman-Peck et al., 2019). Above all, Hannah has been primarily concerned with an analysis of the factors that underpinned the rise of large-scale firms, providing a distinct approach that reflected his commitment to incorporating other social science disciplines, and especially industrial economics, into the analysis. This is perfectly illustrated in *The Rise of the Corporate Economy* (1976) because from the first chapter (Business: history and economics) through to the last (The upshot for welfare) Hannah incorporated economic and quantitative analysis of both merger activity and industrial concentration to chart the evolution of big business in Britain. Crucially, even though in the same year Hannah (1976a) had published the proceedings of a conference designed to analyse Chandler's ideas on business evolution, *The Rise of the Corporate Economy* offered a different approach to that of the Harvard professor by incorporating both internal and external factors in explaining the way in which large-scale British firms grew and adapted. The second edition (1983) proved to be even more significant, in that it included a lot of the data collected for another book written with John Kay, *Concentration in Modern Industry* (1977). This established a highly novel model that many British business historians especially have replicated because in closely analysing British levels of industrial concentration, Hannah and Kay provided fresh insights into key features of the business scene by employing economic techniques, moving the discipline away from its preoccupation with case studies (Foreman-Peck et al., 2019).

While clearly Hannah and the BHU succeeded in providing business history with much greater momentum, it is also clear that the discipline was still capable of missing opportunities. After all, in 1990, Lee was able to publish two essays that were highly critical of business historians' failure to incorporate economic models in their research (Lee, 1990, 1990a). Wilson (1995; pp. 15–19) responded to this *cri de coeur* in his long-term study of British business evolution because in anticipating the later arguments advocated by Kipping et al. (2016), he explained that business historians 'can clearly benefit enormously from extending their awareness of industrial economics' and especially the work of Penrose (1959), Downie (1958) and Marris (1963). At the same time, this work ignored the highly innovative contributions of Andrew Pettigrew to understanding strategic change, reflecting how the discipline as a whole missed another opportunity. Although Reader (1970) had earlier provided a detailed business history of ICI, one of the United Kingdom's most successful twentieth-century companies, Pettigrew (1985) used his studies of strategic decision-making to offer a very different perspective on how one chief executive (John Harvey-Jones) introduced organizational development (OD) techniques into what was by the 1960s and 1970s a highly diversified, multinational operation. The distinctly novel dimension of Pettigrew's work was the way in which he reinterpreted what was often seen as an ahistorical OD process, arguing that it was essential to understand the historical context of each organization undergoing change. To a significant extent, this anticipates the much later work of social scientists such as Suddaby (2010), who as we shall see in Chapter 3.3 introduced concepts such as rhetorical history to explain how organizations utilize their history as a source of competitive advantage. In the late twentieth century, however, business historians almost completely ignored Pettigrew's work, preferring instead to use Reader's narrative (1970).

It would consequently be misleading to claim that by the 1990s British business historians had moved decisively towards the employment of economic concepts in their research. By comparing the articles published in British, American and Japanese business history journals, yet without checking authors' nationality, Lamoreaux et al. (2007) have argued that methodologically they were much more likely to use theory in order to analyse their empirical research. On the other hand, given the failure to accommodate Pettigrew's ideas into work on corporate strategy, it was also clear to many British business historians that a more rigorous approach ought to be developed. Nevertheless, the growing interest amongst British business historians in the application of (industrial) economics to the study of business evolution was a clear reflection of the variety of methodologies that was being employed by the 1990s. Of special note, in this regard, was the growing interest in international business, a field that had initially benefitted enormously from the pioneering work of Wilkins (1970, 1974). Indeed, not only did academics debate the most appropriate economic theory to employ when understanding multinational firms (Lamoreaux et al., 2007), but this also resulted in the participation of leading economists such as Mark Casson at Reading and Peter Buckley at Leeds. While Casson especially developed a close relationship with business historians, when Geoffrey Jones became professor of business history at the University of Reading, they were able to develop a formidable group that has contributed extensively to this literature. Jones would also jointly edit *Business History* with Charles Harvey from 1994 until 2003, further boosting calls for a more extensive application of economic theory in business history research. Although Jones moved to Harvard in 2002, he left a considerable legacy at both Reading and as a leading figure in European business history, contributing extensively to the debate relating to the closer integration of business history into the social sciences (Jones & Khanna, 2006). As we shall see in Chapter 5, other leading international business scholars were also writing enthusiastically about a closer fusion with history, Buckley (2020; p. 797) advocating a 'more critical approach to sources and attention to sequence'. An example of how this could be achieved was Wilson's (1998) application of Dunning's OLI (ownership–location–internalization) paradigm to an analysis of the international strategies developed at Ferranti up to the 1970s. This aligned very closely to the *modus operandi* Jones and Casson had been pursuing since the 1990s, highlighting how that decade was vital in marking a distinctly new era in the development of business history.

The creation of the BHU, and specifically the appointment of Hannah as its inaugural Director, had clearly changed the landscape for business history in the United Kingdom, with significant quantities of public money being invested in both projects and a new generation of academics. As we noted earlier, however, it is important not to ignore the even earlier work at both Liverpool and Glasgow universities, while by the 1990s, business historians had established strong bases in other institutions, especially, Cardiff, Lancaster, Manchester, Reading and Sheffield. The developments in Cardiff were especially notable because an annual workshop eventually evolved into a highly successful journal, *Accounting, Business and Financial History*, which reflected the eclectic manner in which the group approached their research. Led creatively by Richard Edwards and Trevor Boyns, the annual Cardiff workshops provided yet another opportunity for business historians to mix with like-minded scholars and generate fresh approaches.

Another innovative body was the Management History Research Group, founded by Professor Andrew Thomson and several Open University Business School professors who were intent on involving practitioners in their research projects and workshops. Building on this important work, Wilson and Rowlinson used this critical mass to establish another new journal, *Management and Organizational History*, complementing the longer-established *Journal of Management History* by providing a stronger link with organization studies scholars. Wilson and Thomson (2007) also wrote a history of British management that by pursuing a more thematic approach to the topic was intended to provide business school students with a deeper understanding of the way in which British management had evolved. Crucially, business history in the United Kingdom at least was developing both a stronger sense of community and its own distinctive approach to the discipline. Long-term surveys of British business evolution also appeared in the mid-1990s (Wilson, 1995; Jeremy, 1998), while the ABH and EBHA expanded their membership significantly, reflecting the discipline's growing maturity and movement away from the limited Chandlerian approach.[1]

Having noted these important British developments, it is vital to add that in the United States alternative methodologies and approaches to the study of business history were evolving. We noted earlier how Lamoreaux et al. (2003) had highlighted both the vulnerabilities inherent in big business and the dynamism of smaller firms and industrial districts. The latter point also featured heavily in the earlier work of Scranton (1983), an eminent American business historian who was also heavily critical of both Chandler's 'organizational determinism' and especially the excessive focus on large-scale firms (Scranton, 1991). Scranton's study of *Proprietary Capitalism* (1983) highlighted not only the continued prevalence of family owner-managers well into the twentieth century but also the significance of small- and medium-sized firms to the American economy. Above all, Scranton encouraged a genre of business history that not only took into account the internal dynamics of a firm, at whatever scale, but also linked those to the extensive range of influences that would help fashion and determine the success or failure of the enterprise. Specifically, by focusing attention on small firms and industrial districts, Scranton offered a distinctly different view of American business to the Chandlerian model. This approach also linked closely to the expanding global interest in the dynamics inherent in industrial districts and clustering, building on the pioneering work of Piore and Sabel (1984) and Sabel and Zeitlin (1985) that influenced industrial policymakers in many advanced economies, especially after Porter (1990) had advocated clustering as a highly effective way of securing competitive advantage in key growth industries. Scranton's later monographs (1989, 1997) would also significantly assist in 'the effort to rescue family enterprise from the Chandlerian scrapheap' (Lamoreaux et al., 2007; p. 49), a process further boosted by the research of many British business historians (Rose, 1993; Wilson & Popp, 2003).

While through his widely acclaimed publications and conference appearances Scranton was helping significantly to switch the research agendas of many business historians, another branch of his work was as Director of the Hagley Center for the History of Business, Technology and Society from 1992. Apart from editing Studies in Industry and Society, published by Johns Hopkins University Press, Scranton was able to use Hagley's seminar and conference series as another mode of ensuring that a much broader and balanced approach to the study of business history was promulgated. In addition, as Hagley was heavily sponsored by the Du Pont family, Scranton attracted significant numbers of scholars from around the world as Hagley Fellows. Hagley also became the administrative base for the BHC when Roger Horowitz took over as its Secretary, and in 2000, BHC established a new journal, *Enterprise & Society: The International Journal of Business History*, the title of which reveals the intention to broaden business historians' perspectives.

While as we have seen Scranton published a wide array of acclaimed research, of special significance to this survey is *Reimagining Business History* written with renowned French business historian, Patrick Fridenson (Scranton & Fridenson, 2013). Taking fundamental questions such as 'What are historians good for? What are business historians good for?' as their initial challenge, Scranton and Fridenson (2013; p. 2) were intent on directing the discipline towards a much broader range of research than simply analysing the internal dynamics of large-scale corporations. Specifically, they were more interested in 'the challenges of accounting for business *in* history' (2013; p. 3), warning against being lured into various 'traps' such as the 'reification' of specific approaches, and especially the notion that the study of business is dominated by the need to assess the rate of progress towards an ideal view of strategy and structure (2013; pp. 13–15). Specifically, in warning business historians about a variety of 'traps' identified, Scranton and Fridenson (2013; pp. 13–54) argued that it was essential 'to reconnect with multiple streams of research in collateral historical disciplines, and to enrich their stock of conceptual tools'. Building on this exercise, they go on to outline a series of 'opportunities' and 'prospects', leading ultimately to a set of concepts and frameworks that would extend a business historian's toolkit, alongside some resources (or, theoretical concepts) capable of triggering novel and productive questions.

Reimagining Business History has provided many business historians with a much more insightful roadmap in determining how a research project ought to be initiated, and especially in opening the subject up to a much wider range of questions and conclusions. Above all, it challenged what Scranton and Fridenson labelled 'traditional business history (TBH)' (2013; p. 6), which in effect was the Chandlerian model writ large, which ran the acute risk of cutting the discipline off from the study of history proper. Moreover, in extending the remit beyond the industrialized West, they highlighted how people run businesses differently in other parts of the world. This is an issue that Jones (2017) has also tackled when analysing the reasons why business systems in the East differed markedly from those in the West. Scranton was especially concerned to restore contingency to the study of business as well as 'seek[ing] to encourage (and undertake) research that will locate businesses in wider histories and view businesspeople as creating histories, both drawing on cultural practices and generating them' (2013; p. 5). Scranton (2019; 2020) backed up these assertions by moving his academic attention from American firms to those operating in the Communist regimes of Poland and Hungary. Apart from challenging the Western preoccupation with innovation, focusing on the crucial importance of maintenance and repair routines that had already been stressed by the prominent historians of technology Russell and Vinsel (2018), this work revealed fresh insights into the challenge of management in contexts that differed markedly from those in the West, again highlighting the benefits of cross-disciplinary research.

Another field of business history research that has benefited from a closer interaction with other disciplines is corporate governance and corporate networks (Tilba, 2017). Not only has this interaction between legal and governance scholars produced some fresh insights into business evolution, it has also provided opportunities to influence policymakers, given the widespread concern over the last three decades with corporate corruption and fraud. The latter will be illustrated further in Chapter 7, where we will assess the extent to which business history research can influence the way in which corporate governance codes are developed. With specific regard to the research benefits, however, the insights provided by prominent legal scholars such as Cheffins (2008) have considerably augmented our understanding of the divorce between control and ownership in British business. Specifically, Cheffins offered a fresh analytical framework that answered three key questions: Why owners want either to exit or dilute control? Will there be a demand for these shares? And will the new investors be inclined to exercise control? The latter has recently exercised corporate governance scholars extensively, resulting in detailed research into the extent to which institutional investors pursue a disengaged strategy associated with profit maximization (Tilba & Wilson, 2017). With regard to the first two questions, Foreman-Peck and Hannah (2013) have provided even more detail on the divorce between control and ownership prior to 1914, while the extensive work of a team involving Acheson et al. (2015, 2016, 2017, 2019) has unearthed fresh insights into these issues. Interestingly, the latter have succeeded in publishing their research in *The Review of Financial Studies* (2019), while Tilba and Wilson's work (2017) was accepted in the *Journal of Management Studies*, highlighting how business historians and corporate governance scholars can collaborate effectively. The latter have also collaborated on a project to analyse how and why British corporate networks have changed so radically over the last century (Wilson et al., 2018; Buchnea et al., 2020), providing even deeper insights into the governance challenges facing regulators as large firms sought to collude with their peers and financial institutions.

2.4 Conclusions

It is consequently clear that by the early twenty-first century, business history was beginning to break away from the narrow confines imposed by the Chandlerian approach associated with the firm and its organizational dynamics, presenting an extensive challenge to the many business historians who had devoted extensive research time either to refuting Chandler's ideas or confirming their efficacy. As Amatori and Colli (2011; pp. 7–8) noted in their highly challenging and thematic study of business evolution while acknowledging the contributions Chandler made to moving business history into a more central position within the social sciences, the discipline needed to move out of his shadow and elaborate more ambitious perspectives that accommodated both internal and external dimensions influencing both business evolution and its wider impact. While one might claim that this reflected what had been happening in the discipline since the 1990s, and especially the work on international business (Jones, 1996) and industrial districts (Wilson & Popp, 2003; Popp & Wilson, 2007), the contributions of Amatori and Colli (2011) and of Scranton and Fridenson (2013) reflected a maturing across business history that was born out in the rapidly expanding literature on the subject and increased attendance at dedicated conferences.

Of course, this summary does not do full justice to the extensive development of business history across many countries. The Business

History Society of Japan had been in existence since 1964, arising from the pioneering work of Keichiro Nakagawa. By 2021, it had over 800 members, running highly popular conferences and workshops, including the Fuji Conference which aims to encourage exchanges between Japanese and overseas scholars. The *Japan Business History Review (Keieishigaku)* is also published four times a year in Japanese, alongside the English journal *Japan Research in Business History*, contributing extensively to understanding the evolution of Japanese business. Other notable developments have been the establishment in 1999 of a Centre for Business History at Copenhagen Business School, focusing especially on the role and impact of business in society. As an integral part of one of the world's leading business schools, this Centre has made a significant impact on business history in Europe, generating an impressive range of publications and attracting scholars from many parts of the world. One must also mention Gesellschaft für Unternehmensgeschichte e. V. (GUG), which was established in 1976 by several leading corporations and some prominent academics. As we shall see in Chapter 8, by expanding its membership to individuals in the 1990s, it rapidly became one of Europe's most active centres for the study and dissemination of business history, contributing extensively to the further development of the EBHA, and later the World Congress of Business Historians (Geschichte der GUG (unternehmensgeschichte. de)). There were also parallel developments at prestigious universities in Barcelona, Milan (Bocconi) and Oslo (BI Norwegian Business School), ensuring that business history from the 1990s especially was globally acknowledged as a discipline in its own right, emerging from the shadows of economic history as that discipline went into a steep decline and business historians looked in increasing numbers for job security in business schools.

As we shall now go on to assess, however, the discipline's credibility outside its own confines was still limited. As Álvaro-Moya and Donzé (2016; p. 124) note: 'Even if business history is a discipline at the crossroads between history and management science, most of the scholars involved in this field are historians...Historians' lack of interest in generalization, conceptualization and theorization led also to the disinterest of management scholars'. This inevitably poses a challenge to business historians, and especially those who pursue careers in either business schools or other social science departments. On the other hand, Scranton and Fridenson (2013; p. 8) see this as an opportunity to 'reconnect with multiple streams of research in collateral historical disciplines', highlighting how over the last decade a major debate has emerged between those who advocated closer links with the social sciences and historians who regarded this as a dilution of what historians ought to be doing. An indication of the discipline's status was the inclusion of business history in the Oxford University Press's *Handbook* series (Jones & Zeitlin, 2007; p. 1), bringing together a distinguished group of American and European scholars to provide 'a state-of-the-art survey of research'. At the same time, with the exception of chapters by Kipping and Üsdiken and by Lipartito, this collection highlighted what over the following decades were to be the dual challenges to business history as a discipline, namely, the failure both to develop a clear methodological direction and fully incorporate social science theory into research projects. The traditional approach to business history had also been highlighted two years earlier when Jeremy and Tweedale (2005; pp. xxi–xxii) claimed:

> Business history is about what we understand to have occurred in the past. It is not primarily an exercise in defending or assaulting currently-fashionable management theories, though they may inform interpretation of the evidence of the past. The historian's first task is to establish the facts of the matter. Facts based on reliable evidence will keep the historian close to the realities of the past, provide accurate chronology, and thus help to ensure the perception of logical cause-and-effect relationships.

Of course, historians generally can be accused of exactly the same approach, eschewing the need for methodology and theory in favour of empirical research based on a detailed assessment and analysis of available sources. Increasingly, though, business historians were coming into contact with social scientists in business schools and associated conferences, providing an intellectual context that would prove highly challenging. At the same time, social scientists were showing a much greater interest in history as an essential feature of their research, a subject we shall move on to assess in the next chapter. In spite of the critiques offered by many prominent scholars, however, as Rowlinson and Delahaye (2009; p. 90) conclude: 'Business history proper remains resolutely empiricist and atheoretical in the sense that its conceptualizations and claims are relatively unexamined and it lacks an ostentatiously theoretical language'.

Note

1 For a fuller history of the ABH, see Association of Business Historians (abh-net.org).

3 Business history and the 'historic turn'

3.1 Introduction

Interest in the use of historical methods and sources has increased dramatically since the 'historic turn' that influenced the discipline of organization studies after Clark and Rowlinson (2004) produced their watershed article. Of course, there had been many earlier suggestions that social scientists ought to pay more attention to longitudinal matters (Zald, 1993; Kieser, 1994) but only after 2004 did this debate begin to embrace business historians. Crucially, though, it is worth examining exactly what kind of 'historic turn' had occurred and whether the 'history' that is argued as being of potential value to organization studies is the same as the empirically based history that has been performed traditionally by business historians. Furthermore, if the history of the 'historic turn' is different in its approach to the kind of business history that this book professes to be espousing, then it raises the question of how and whether business history and business historians have contributed to the debate. This also highlights a recurring theme of the book, namely, the extent to which business history needs to align with the social sciences in order to gain greater credibility. It will certainly become clear that the discipline has been heavily influenced by this 'historic turn' debate, with many of its leading protagonists devoting considerable attention to experimenting with applications of social science theory to historical research, while similarly social scientists have produced exciting new genres such as 'rhetorical history'. This chapter will track the emergence of the 'historic turn' and its impact on business history through the emergence of these fresh approaches, incorporating the uses of the past, corporate archives, and the most recent developments in what has been labelled 'historical organization studies' (HOS).

DOI: 10.4324/9780429449536-3

3.2 The historic turn

Organization studies scholars had begun making calls for the reintegration of history and historical methods within the discipline in the early 1990s, with Zald (1993) and Kieser (1994) criticizing organization studies as a discipline for its lack of a longitudinal perspective. Both criticized the discipline's drive to create generalizable theory, with Zald (1993; p. 515) stating that 'many of the very generalisable theoretical schemas have come to nought. They have crashed on the shoals of banality'. Kieser (1994; p. 609) also noted that 'structures of and behaviours in organizations reflect culture-specific historical developments. Differences between organizations in different cultures can, therefore, only be explained completely if the historical dimension is included in the comparison'. Both scholars argued that organization studies could benefit from opening itself up to historical methods and ideas in generating new ideas, questioning the positivist mindset that dominated the discipline and open up scholars to the value of other forms of organizing that might have failed in the past but could be of value in the present (Zald, 1993; pp. 519–521; Kieser, 1994; p. 610).

This call for a greater use of historical methods and historical sources was later captured by Clark and Rowlinson (2004) in their seminal article demanding a 'historic turn' in organization studies. Clark and Rowlinson argued that a real transformation in organization studies would:

> [R]epresent a turn *against* the view that organization studies should constitute a branch of the science of society. [...] Second, as in other fields, an historic turn would involve "a contentious and by no means well-defined turn *towards* [emphasis in original] history – as past, process, contest and so on" [but not] necessarily towards the most adjacent branch of history, which is the case of organization studies would be business history. Finally, an historic turn would entail a turn to the historiographical debates and historical theories of interpretation that recognise the inherent ambiguity of the term 'history' itself … This would necessitate greater reflection on the place of historical narrative in organization studies.
>
> (Clark & Rowlinson, 2004; p. 331)

Engagement with historiographical questions would have the effect of revealing the subjectivity of the narratives presented in case studies, a common teaching tool in business schools, undermining the 'ready-made lessons learned from history' they present (Clark & Rowlinson, 2004; p. 347). At the same time, Clark and Rowlinson warn that organization studies scholars remain suspicious of the use of historical narratives based on a Foucauldian aversion to the imposition of narratives on history and a preference for general theories over context-specific ones. To combat this, Clark and Rowlinson point towards the value of historical methods and data in the work of Alfred Chandler and Andrew Pettigrew as examples of the benefits such an approach can bring.

By the time of Clark and Rowlinson's article, work had already been produced on how organizations used their past to build organizational culture. Ooi (2002) and Rowlinson and Hassard (1993) showed how organizations shape their historical narratives to produce emotional effects in targeted audiences. Parker (2002) also notes, however, that an organization's historical narrative is not only created by managers, but it is also co-constructed and shaped by a variety of stakeholders who hold different understandings of its history. Furthermore, organizations focus on remembering, or forgetting, particular events to shape the identity of the organization (Gioia et al., 2002; Nissley & Casey, 2002).

3.3 Rhetorical history

Some of the most influential early works on how organizations use their past introduced the idea of *rhetorical history*. Focusing on institutional change in the Canadian accounting and legal services industries that would bring together accounting and legal services within the same provider, work by Suddaby and Greenwood (2005) showed how history could be a potent rhetorical resource for both those arguing in favour and against such change as well as their efforts to legitimize, or de-legitimize, the change. History was used in various ways by both sides, highlighting historical continuity as a reason to oppose changes to a system that works; or instead, it could suggest that the changes being sought were in line with the past and, therefore, not to be feared. Of the 121 instances of historical arguments being used, 48% were against the proposed changes, while 52% were used to support them, showing how history was such a malleable resource for both sides.

Suddaby built on this work, coining the term rhetorical history to 'capture the notion that history can be an affective managerial tool within organizations', and defining it as 'the strategic use of the past as a persuasive strategy to manage key stakeholders of the firm' (Suddaby et al., 2010; p. 157). Rhetorical history drew on various strands of organization studies scholarship, including storytelling in organizations, organizational memory and organizational identity. In turn, earlier organization studies scholarship was criticized for its approach to the study of history, arguing that earlier research had often treated history as an objective series of events that an organization has experienced, such as in the work of Stinchcombe (1965) and his idea of imprinting, or with the concept of path dependency (David, 1985). Both imprinting and path dependency are closer to what historians understood as the past – namely, an objective series of events – which differed from history which is understood as the narratives that were constructed to make sense of past events (Suddaby et al., 2010; pp. 150–156).

As we noted earlier, organization studies scholars had already begun producing work that highlighted how organizations use historical narratives to manage stakeholders' perceptions (Rowlinson & Hassard, 1993; Nissley & Casey, 2002; Ooi, 2002). Other scholars later added to this body of work, for example, Booth et al.'s (2007) study of the German publisher Bertelsmann which had constructed a corporate history portraying it as an honourable company that had opposed Hitler and the Nazi regime, a narrative that fitted their contemporary corporate identity but did not align with the historical facts. This instance of 'strategic forgetting' mirrors Nissley and Casey's (2002) discussion of the politics of memory at play in organizational memory. 'Strategic forgetting' has been used by organizations to depict them in a more favourable light, as Anteby and Molnar (2012) showed with their study of Snecma, a French aeronautics firm. Snecma repeatedly hid its reliance on German expertise and collaboration with German companies after World War Two in order not to damage its connection with the French reconstruction project. These works showed how organizational historical narratives are often constructed with the contemporary context in mind, directing what is/is not remembered in a way that historians would regard as ahistorical.

Establishing the legitimacy of an organization or industry is another way that organizations have used rhetorical history narratives. Organizations, such as fine wine producers in Ontario, Canada, used rhetorical history narratives to appear legitimate to other audiences such as customers, critics and competitors (Hills et al., 2013; Voronov et al., 2013). These wine producers utilized rhetorical history narratives to distance themselves from harmful associations such as their relative youth, especially when compared to 'Old World' wines, linking themselves to prevailing industry logics to appear more legitimate. Other examples of this manipulation of history showed how organizations used rhetorical history narratives to brand both their products and the firm to appeal to audiences. Studies showed how companies, such as Absolut Vodka (Ooi, 2002), Tim Hortons (Foster et al., 2011), German watchmakers (Oertel & Thommes, 2015), Colt (Poor et al., 2016) and Jack Daniel's (Holt, 2006), have all used rhetorical history narratives as a method of branding and constructing their corporate identity. These historical narratives are not necessarily factually accurate and instead draw from larger historical themes and ideas that are present in the audiences they are targeting, such as national myths and symbols (Foster et al., 2011; Poor et al., 2016), or regional historical narratives that help to associate the product or brand with particular ideas such as high-quality products (Oertel & Thommes, 2015).

Companies have also used their history to promote strategic change, such as Procter & Gamble's (P&G) use of its history as a resource to manage change within the company, establishing the continuity of the organization's history and values, but also allowing for reinterpretation and change as the organization grew, and thereby minimizing resistance (Maclean et al., 2014). Additionally, in times of crisis, an organization's history can be a potent resource for reimagining its corporate identity and strategy, as was the case with Adidas (Iglesias et al., 2020) and Lego (Schultz & Hernes, 2013). The use of historical narratives to both implement and inhibit change can also occur within the same organization at the same time. This has been documented by Ybema (2014), focusing on editors at a Dutch newspaper, and Brunninge (2009), on Scania and Handelsbanken, a Swedish vehicle manufacturer and bank, respectively. At the same time, historical narratives can also act as an impediment to change, as has been the case with Danish savings banks (Hansen, 2007) and in attempts to change North American lighting standards (McGaughey, 2013). These works once again highlight the malleability of history as a resource for the various actors who used it, both promoting and inhibiting change, depending on the situation and the actors involved.

Research on how organizations use the past has also grown out of the rhetorical history literature. The popularity of categorizing work as 'rhetorical history' rather than as 'uses of the past' is based on a search of the keywords used to describe articles on SAGE's website, the publishers of *Organization Studies* in partnership with the European Group for Organization Studies (EGOS). A search for 'rhetorical history' from 1997 to 2021 responds with fifty articles ('Sage Journals', n.d.-a); the same search using 'uses of the past' returns eighteen results ('Sage Journals', n.d.-b). If the search is narrowed to 2018–2021, the year a special issue was published on the subject, the searches return eighteen results for 'rhetorical history' ('Sage Journals', n.d.-c) and eight for 'uses of the past' ('Sage Journals', n.d.-d).

While the uses of the past and rhetorical history approaches have opened new avenues for research on how organizations deploy their historical resources, it has been critiqued by some scholars for how it 'elides the differences between history and memory' (Decker et al., 2020). This critique is pertinent to whether business history and business historians can contribute to this research agenda, given that business history is an empirically based discipline that focuses on understanding how businesses interact with and influence the world around them. As Decker et al. (2020) argue, historians have often defined history as a knowledge of the past constructed from the traces of the past left behind and distinct from the past itself, whereas memory has been defined as the 'invocation of the past in the present ... designed to create an atemporal sense of the past in the present' (Katriel, 1994, as cited in Decker et al., 2020; p. 6). The uses of the past approach, with its view of history as an 'ongoing set of practices through which the past is used to help actors make sense of the present and imagine the future' (Wadhwani et al., 2018; p. 1667), are consequently more akin to previous definitions of memory than history, a criticism that could equally be applied to rhetorical history. This merging of the concepts of history and memory could well hide the different ways they are used in organizations and the ways they transform into one another (Foroughi et al., 2020). It also potentially ignores the contributions of history as a discipline – with its established methods for generating knowledge of the past – by only focusing on historical narratives as things to be studied to understand their construction, rather than valid methods of presenting research findings and their potential contributions to knowledge or theory.

The uses of the past and rhetorical history literature, as well as the 'historic turn' approach more generally, have also recently come under intense criticism for their approach towards studying history. Much of this criticism focuses on the postmodern epistemology on which the 'historic turn' literature is based as well as how it has interpreted some of its key philosophical influences. Bowden (2018; pp. 214–231) argues that much of this literature rarely directly references its key scholars or discusses the ontological and epistemological positions that directly affect how the study of history should be performed. This lack of specificity and reflection leads to scholars being cited as key inspirations for uses of the past approaches despite the scholars in question holding different positions on epistemology. For Bowden (2020; p. 22), 'the holding of confused and contradictory positions is not an accidental by-product of the "historic turn", rather, it is a defining characteristic of the genre'.

Bowden (2018; p. 214) also criticizes proponents of the 'historic turn' for misrepresenting what historians do and the sources they use, while presenting their interpretations of how history should be researched as accepted fact. Historians that do not follow postmodern approaches to the study of history are dismissed as 'positivists', with critics citing Von Ranke as influencing historians to take an approach to history which promotes writing history as it really was (Bowden, 2018; p. 229, 2020; p. 23). Apart from this being a misreading of Ranke's position, Bowden (2018; p. 230) also argues that this unfairly portrays historians as 'naive and unreflective fools' when faced with textual sources and ignoring the wide range of sources that historians use. As Toms and Wilson (2010; p. 112) show, business historians do not just use textual sources because material can also be derived from 'price data and other numerical evidence, accounting records, archaeological remains, film records, Internet [sic] sources and so on'. Although Toms and Wilson were responding specifically to calls for business history to incorporate Ricoeur's approach (Taylor et al., 2009), this does call into question whether the postmodern approaches advocated by the 'historic turn' are applicable to all forms of historical sources and analysis.

Connected to these criticisms regarding the nature of evidence and what historians do are accusations that postmodernist-inspired approaches can lead to inaccurate history. This critique can best be seen in two reviews of *A New History of Management* (Cummings et al., 2017). Both Batiz-Lazo (2019) and Muldoon (2019) praise the ambition of the book, which revisits the management history that has been told in textbooks since the early 1970s. On the other hand, both critique the volume for ignoring context, particularly in relation to their interpretation of Adam Smith and his views on slavery, taxation and the context of the political situation in which he was writing (Batiz-Lazo, 2019; pp. 117–118; Muldoon, 2019; pp. 130–131). While much of the criticism of the volume is specific to the book itself, Batiz-Lazo and Muldoon extend their critiques to the approach more generally. Batiz-Lazo (2019; p. 122) states that the book suffers some of the 'most common short-comings of "critical management" research, namely leaving a conceptual and empirical void after an elaborated critique', arguing that 'constructive criticism is more than telling people what they have done wrong but indicating clear pathways for them to do better'. Muldoon (2019; p. 133) is perhaps more scathing: 'As a work of history, this book is a failure – perhaps, the best argument to make is that is it an ANTi-history book. It fails because the authors do not apply the craft of history'. These failings, Muldoon (2019; p. 133) asserts, are due to their postmodernist approach 'to whom everything is based on politics and power', whereas 'historical evidence is based on probability through a careful weighing of the evidence'.

As we can see from this review, from its outset rhetorical history focused on different phenomena from traditional business history and was founded on a different epistemological basis. Rather than trying to understand the past through the study of an organization or industry's routines, structures and practices over time, rhetorical history focuses on different phenomena, namely, how an organization remembers and uses its past as a resource in the present. Rather than making claims about the past, the rhetorical history literature deconstructs historical narratives to show how they were constructed and for what purposes they are used, highlighting how discourse analysis provides a core methodology for those who advocate this approach.

Despite the differences, this is arguably a field where business historians and organization studies scholars need to come together to conduct the research. As Suddaby (2016) argues, the value of history for organizations is its power to 'convey social and symbolic capital – that is authenticity, legitimacy, and reputation – to the corporation', while at the same time, 'its capacity to perform these functions is directly linked to the structural objective elements of history as fact' (Suddaby, 2016; p. 54). Understanding how organizations use history consequently requires the skills of historians who can compare the ways historical research is performed by academics with the ways that organizations have used history to construct their historical narratives. Indeed, this distinction is potentially an important contribution to the benefit of non-historians in order to strengthen the distinction between, on the one hand, history as knowing the past, the approach of academic historians, as opposed to representing the past through historical narratives, the 'myth-making' approach of organizations (Decker, 2016; p. 374).

Rhetorical history research, properly supported by business historians, can also act as a check on organizations, ensuring their historical narratives are factually accurate and do not gloss over historical misdeeds. If rhetorical history narratives are concerned with the underlying historical truth that is being used by organizations, then this would also suggest that there remains a place for traditional business history research to act as a key source for rhetorical history research against which one can compare organizational history narratives. Of course, this requires agreement on how to conduct historical research between business historians and uses of the past scholars with different ontological and epistemological positions on what constitutes history and historical truth. Such an agreement will likely require historians to continue to defend their methods and approaches as rigorous, while at the same time being more explicit in what they are (Decker, 2013), so as to justify their interpretation as a more accurate narrative of the past than that put forward by organizations. This clarification of methods would also allow non-historians to be more confident in justifying their use of those narratives in their own research (Coraiola et al., 2015). At the same time, those who take a position that views history as interpretation and construction would need to accept that the work of historians is not the same history as that performed by organizations. Despite the biases and power structures that might influence the construction of a historical narrative, the work of professional historians is likely to be more reflective of the events of the past as they happened when compared to how an organization presents itself. If business historians are to make the effort to be clearer about the methods that underpin their findings and potential biases in their findings, it is also necessary for organization studies scholars to accept that historical methods and narratives are valid ways of conducting and presenting research.

3.4 Historical organization studies

Building on the increased interaction between organization studies and business history is the recent emergence of the highly creative school of HOS. This approach was initiated by Maclean et al. (2016), who designed HOS to perform research where 'history is integral, in which history and organization studies are of equal status, underpinned by the notion of *dual integrity*, as opposed to the history of a specific organization or set of organizational circumstances' (Maclean et al., 2016; p. 612, italics in original). Although recognizing that these are separate disciplines, albeit oriented to the study of the same phenomena, the focus on 'dual integrity' requires that the research is authentic to both disciplines, spanning the boundaries and avoiding one becoming subsidiary to the other. For business historians, this means that the research has *historical veracity*, that the resulting narrative 'rings true' (Maclean et al., 2016; p. 625) and is faithful to the evidence, that sources are clearly referenced and that the interpretation of sources is logical and consistent with the evidence provided.

With regard to organization studies, authenticity lies in the research adding to theory development and that it contributes to generalizable knowledge within the field.

Maclean et al. (2016) discuss four potential contributions that HOS can make to organization studies and business history: evaluating theory through testing it against historical data; explicating historical events by the application of theory to historical processes, thereby gaining a deeper understanding of both; conceptualizing new theory, or developing existing theory, using historical data and constructing narratives that contain detailed discussions of phenomena which can be the basis for detailed analysis. Although Maclean et al. (2016) recognize that Suddaby's (2010) earlier work on rhetorical history and the study of Andrew Carnegie by Harvey et al. (2011) demonstrated similar approaches to HOS, through their work at EGOS in developing a dedicated sub-theme ensured that their methodology became widely accepted. This was reflected in a recent book that demonstrates various approaches to HOS in practice (Maclean et al., 2020; Mutch, 2020; Sakai, 2020) and approach (Chihadeh, 2020; Durepos & Vince, 2020). Additionally, Durepos et al. (2020) use the principles of HOS as a way of categorizing the submission to a special issue of *Management Learning*, highlighting the potential contributions that could be made by scholars who seek to engage with HOS and historical methods and sources. Scholars have also shown how a HOS approach can develop existing theory. For example, Thompson's (2018) study of the impact of digital music distribution on record pooling practice in the United States develops neo-institutionalist theory, while research by Luyckx and Janssens (2016) shows how a HOS approach can develop theory on discursive legitimation strategies.

Having stressed the novelty associated with HOS's principle of dual integrity, however, it is possible that this approach could well become the preserve of a few academics that have the elusive combination of theoretical fluency and the skills of a historian. This highlights the vital necessity to ensure that there is effective collaboration between business historians and organization scholars. Without collaboration of this kind, HOS could well become the preserve of one discipline over another. Indeed, as Decker et al. (2020) point out, much current HOS research has been more interested in advancing organization studies theory, rather than advancing the understanding of the past. Moreover, HOS does not always appreciate the limitations that using historical events to advance contemporary theory can create, highlighting in graphic form how there is an acute risk of business history being subsumed into organization studies, rather than acting as a bridge to connect the two. Additionally, while business historians would appear to be well placed to contribute to this form of co-operation, given their location in business schools, journals that are primarily focused towards organization studies have been averse to publishing research that utilizes historical methods or sources (Leblebici, 2014; Suddaby, 2016). Although the recent special issues discussed in Chapter 4 suggest that this attitude is beginning to change, it remains the case that organization studies scholars and business historians need to devote scarce research time to projects that might not be publishable in journals important to their field, with unclear consequences for careers and job performance measurement. Clearly, then, while HOS has the potential to integrate organization studies and business history in a way that contributes to both fields (Decker et al., 2020; Maclean et al., 2020), it will consequently require the sustained and coordinated effort of academics from both disciplines as well as the willingness of journal editors at influential journals to publish work that uses historical methods and sources.

3.5 ANTi-history

Building on the work of Bruno Latour (1987) with Actor-Network Theory (ANT), another innovative approach that has recently emerged is what has been labelled ANTi-history (Durepos & Mills, 2011). Similar to rhetorical history, ANTi-history often takes the historical narrative as the object of study, rather than the events of the past. Unlike rhetorical history, however, ANTi-history does not study how managers have attempted to use historical narratives – although such actions could well be of interest – but instead analyses how knowledge of the past is produced and how the dominant narrative became the legitimate one over time due to the actions of various individuals, organizations, institutions and objects. More specifically, ANTi-history analyses the relationality between actors and networks, including non-human actors such as books, records, archives and other objects, highlighting how certain narratives gain legitimacy over others, and in the process calling into question extant understandings and knowledge. While this methodology understands the past as an objective series of events, it also sees history as socially constructed knowledge of the past that is based on actors' attempts to understand and define it, with historical narratives based on evidence that is itself non-human actors that are remnants of previously existing networks (Durepos & Mills, 2011).

The real value in this approach is the way in which it is argued that historical narratives are a socially constructed knowledge of the past;

historians do not study history but 'do history' (Durepos & Mills, 2011; p. 711) and therefore make active political choices when choosing what to (and not to) represent. For Durepos and Mills (2011; p. 716), historians should not attempt to 'capture the past as it happened', as this helps to maintain the social domination of particular groups over others; instead, historians should strive to construct a multiplicity of historical narratives, highlighting that any one narrative is merely a choice of interpretation rather than the objective truth, in turn 'liberating actors from otherwise dominant interpretations of the socio-past'. To do this, ANTi-history scholarship strives to show both the historical narrative that conveys both the findings and how this narrative came to be, disclosing the relationship between the writers' political and social tactics and the resulting research (Durepos & Mills, 2018). This demonstrates how ANTi-history can facilitate a more deliberate approach to history along the lines Durepos and Mills (2012) suggest by bringing to light the social processes that have led to the privileging of one narrative over others and, in their view, how historical knowledge is socially created.

ANTi-history has been used to show the processes that underpin the creation of official corporate histories, bringing to the surface the discussions and decisions that were required to construct the narrative, but that are often hidden by it, giving it the appearance of 'an uncontested representation of the past' (Durepos et al., 2008; p. 64). Focusing on Pan American Airlines (Pan Am), they document how the company's official history was created, heavily influenced by the actions of the company's President and Vice President, who not only decided who would author it but also collected the material that formed Pan Am's early archives and even wrote large sections of the book before a professional author could be found who would agree to the company's terms. Focusing on another airline, Coller et al. (2016) show how the construction of British Airways' (BA) archives affected the historical narratives that were dominant in the organization. Rather than focusing only on the contents of the archive, however, Coller et al. also consider the effect of human actors, such as archivists and historians, and their relationships with one another when analysing how the archive's construction has influenced, and been influenced by, pre-existing historical narratives. These activities have resulted in a dominant narrative that is gendered, in that it predominantly focuses on the achievements of male pilots, business expansion and technological progress, presenting BA's past as an unbroken line from 1919, instead of discussing the various companies that preceded it or were merged into it.

Other scholars have shown how historical narratives that were the result of negotiations between actors could well have been important in legitimizing an organization. Myrick et al. (2013) trace the devilment of the Academy of Management's (AOM) historical narrative, in particular, its claim to have been founded in 1936, a claim that gave it increased legitimacy in its formative years, ignoring the several discontinuities that occurred. Alternatively, multiple historical narratives can be used to understand marginalized communities, as Corrigan (2016) shows. Utilizing the decisions of state-level budgetary accountants, Corrigan documents three historical narratives of Africville, a town formed by escaped slaves, Black Loyalists, and free Blacks in Halifax, Nova Scotia, in the early nineteenth century and destroyed in the 1960s following forced rehousing of the community. The three narratives were one of neglect, the refusal by budgeters to allocate money for basic services to a town that would not raise sufficient tax revenue to cover them and was seen as 'a problem' (Corrigan, 2016; p. 90); one of aggression, where money was allocated to Africville, but for projects that damaged the town and were unwanted elsewhere, such as sewage pits, prisons and freight train tracks and a romantic narrative that has reimagined Africville as a picturesque seaside town destroyed unfairly and deserving to be remembered. All these narratives resulted in real-world consequences as actors were enrolled in the networks, such as the lack of funding for basic services, the destruction of the town, and funding for an Africville museum and class action lawsuit demanding reparations for former residents. This work shows how multiple interpretations of the past can all be true, and the enrolment of actors into networks shapes their actions, potentially further marginalizing some groups or creating demands for justice.

Of course, ANTi-history is not without its critics. While some of these critiques are similar to those related above with regard to the historic turn and use of the past approach, there are issues specific to ANTi-history that scholars such as Muldoon (2020) and Bowden (2020) highlight. For both scholars, ANTi-history has an almost 'conspiratorial' (Muldoon, 2020; p. 98) view of human nature and activity, Muldoon (2020) arguing that in his experience archivists are not prone to altering the historical record purposely, rather than preserving as much as possible, warts and all. Likewise, Bowden (2020; p. 20) argues that organizations are too concerned with short-term survival to tailor records in an effort to enrol others into its network. While organizations certainly create records primarily concerned with enrolling others, such as advertising material or annual reports, day-to-day records often tell a different story and are regularly used by historians to show, as accurately as possible, what was actually happening at an organization.

In addition, these critics disagree with the implied view of historians that ANTi-history posits, namely, that they are at the mercy of the current dominant political thinking. While Bowden (2020) agrees that historians are affected by biases, he argues that historians have varied political opinions that change over time in accordance with the evidence presented. Similarly, Muldoon (2020) states that historians are well aware of the bias inherent in both their thinking and their sources; indeed, this is an inherent feature of historical research. Although awareness of these biases does not mean the eradication of them in one's own work, to argue that a historian is merely an 'ideologue' (Bowden, 2020; p. 21) for the dominant politics of the day does a disservice to the level of reflectivity and variety of scholarship in the discipline. Another of Bowden's (2020) critiques is connected to ANTi-history's view of the historian as it calls for historians to view their work as 'an impactful vehicle to enact a leftist ideology' (Durepos et al., 2020; p. 454). For Bowden (2020; p. 21), this conflicts with the purposes of academic research, namely, that researchers can 'look beyond their own preconceived notions to be guided by the evidence' in a search for truth wherever it takes them.

The debates relating to the applicability of ANTi-history will no doubt continue, again revealing how business history has not only recently attracted scholars from many different fields but also offers a fresh approach to studying historical narratives, offering different insights to that of rhetorical history or traditional business history. By showing how historical knowledge is created and accepted as legitimate, it demands that historians ought to pay attention to the choices they make when conducting research. Additionally, by showing how historical narratives can affect decision-making with potentially damaging outcomes, it can act as a warning to managers who intend to use the past as a resource that they must be judicious in how they do this in order to avoid one-sided narratives that create problems in the future. As an additional boon to historians, ANTi-history effectively calls for more historical research to be conducted as it calls for multiple narratives of the same events, albeit with the caveat that this research should be conducted differently from how it has been done in the past. While ANTi-history is not without its critics, for historians willing to adopt this approach, it can offer the opportunity to increase the reach of their work to those sceptical of historical research within organization studies, demonstrating their rigour, how difficult choices are made and the logic that underpins the creation of historical knowledge.

3.6 Corporate uses of the archive

How organizations make use of their archives is another recent strand of research that has developed as the interest in how organizations use their pasts has grown. Interest in the nature and use of corporate archives by their parent organizations is not a new topic; in Britain, the Business Archives Council (BAC) was officially founded in 1934 and transformed its newsletter *Business Archives* into a serious academic journal in the 1960s, increasing the number of publications per year until splitting it into two in 1987, *Principles and Practices* and *Sources and History* (Anson, 2010). In the United States, interest in corporate archives began to grow as business history developed following the formation of the Business History Society in 1925 (Cook, 1926). In 1982, a special issue of *The American Archivist* was published, in part, to recognize the widespread interest in corporate archives and celebrate the growth in their number (Anderson, 1982). This body of literature has discussed many ways in which organizations benefit from their archival holdings, both for their historical value and, perhaps more importantly in terms of their continued survival, their contemporary value to an organization (Gardner, 1982; Mooney, 1982; Rabchuk, 1997; Lasewicz, 2015). These purposes include preserving authentic records that can be used to support a range of activities, including compliance with regulatory requirements or in legal proceedings (Mooney, 1993; Gray, 2002; D. C. Force, 2014); as a source of publicity or material for advertising and corporate communications (Markley, 2008; M. Force, 2009; Kemal Ataman, 2009); inspiring the creation of new brands and products (Aohi, 2012) and constructing an organizational identity (Bieri, 2012; Hagund Tousey, 2012; Pino, 2012).

Despite this body of literature, corporate archives have generally been left unstudied by organization studies scholars, possibly due to the preference in social sciences to construct data sets, rather than rely on archival data (Rowlinson et al., 2014; Yates, 2014). This reveals one of the fundamental differences between historians and social scientists, in that while the latter classify data generated from their own research as primary, the former would regard sources such as archives, newspapers and public sources as primary.

While business historians have often discussed the drawbacks of having to rely on corporate archives (Hannah, 1983; Coleman, 1987), until recently they had rarely explicitly analysed how and why archives are constructed. This omission was more often due to the failure of historians to be explicit about the methodologies they employ, rather than a lack of understanding of how an archive has been constructed and its influence on their research (Fellman & Popp, 2013). It is never-theless true that the 'historic turn' and rising interest in how organizations use their history has led to a greater interest in how corporate archives are constructed, for what purposes they are maintained and how organizations make use of them, all questions that historical methods might be best placed to answer (Wadhwani et al., 2018).

Business historians have contributed to this discussion by more clearly explaining how they use corporate archives and the problems that scholars might encounter. Fellman and Popp (2013) used interviews with other business historians and reflect on their own experiences to highlight the practical difficulties of working with corporate archives, offering suggestions on how these can be overcome. Decker (2013) takes a different approach, instead highlighting the impact of post-colonial theory on how business historians approach archives in post-colonial countries and deal with the silences in the archive. Further work by Popp and Fellman (2020) has exposed the gross power imbalances when utilizing corporate archives. Taking a stakeholder perspective, they chart four interest groups – owners, audiences, professional historians and archivists – and their relative power and interest over archival holdings. While other scholars have noted the problems with relying on corporate archives, Popp and Fellman's (2020) contribution allows for a more nuanced understanding of how the corporate archive is used and controlled by a variety of stakeholders, making it an object worthy of study in itself.

Other scholars have researched how organizations make use of their archives as part of their uses of the past activities and strategies. For example, Smith and Simeone (2017) show how the Hudson Bay Company's (HBC) decision to construct a corporate archive in 1928 was tied to their increasing use of rhetorical history narratives and the need to ensure they were perceived as legitimate. On the other hand, Hatch and Shultz (2017) show how employees at the Carlsberg Group utilized its corporate archives as inspiration for a new line of products based around the history of craft brewing at the company. This approach was inspired by the phrase *Semper Ardens* (always burning) carved in the doorway above the Group's historical headquarters. They later used the corporate archives to find further inspiration for both the branding and recipes for new product lines, demonstrating how the use of the archives and historical symbols helped to give the product line a degree of authenticity it may have otherwise lacked. This use of archives as inspiration for historically authentic products is also used in other industries, Vacca (2014) showing how fashion companies use their museums and archives as both a means of promotion and a source of inspiration. Similarly, Castellani and Rossato (2014; p. 247) demonstrate the application of corporate archives and museums to the construction of corporate identity, allowing for the 'immediacy of transferring messages through actual experience'. This highlights how corporate museums and archives allow the company to show the values and identity of the firm as well as 'embody a complete form of communication through the viewing of objects, listening to the accounts, touching, smelling and tasting the product' (2014; p. 247). Although museums and archives are different in their purpose and operation, both allow organizations to communicate with local communities and demonstrate the local history they share.

Another area in which corporate archives might also be useful is the way in which they can be applied to managerial decision-making and strategy formulation. Scholars have argued previously that looking to the past, particularly the distant past, can be useful in developing strategy, given the way that it can encourage managers to plan further into the future than more recent events (Schultz & Hernes, 2013). How managers access the past has been discussed less often, as it would stand to reason that the types of resources they use to look to the past would affect their decision-making. Van Lent and Smith (2019) theorize that corporate archives might prove to be a useful resource for managers when engaging in sense-making and analogical reasoning, comparing similar events to each other to understand their similarities and differences. When managers do not have sufficient experience or knowledge of the past, they can draw on archival evidence to assess their current circumstances, given that it can prove to be a useful repository of historical events and produce emotional reactions in employees and help to mobilize action.

The corporate use of the archive would appear to be an area in which the experience of business historians should enable them to make a substantial contribution. Historians have experience working with archival sources, while business historians in particular have experience in using corporate archival records and navigating the interests of various stakeholders to produce historical research. This work will often extend to building relationships with the organizations studied and the archivists who have enabled their research. These types of relationships can be crucial in persuading both the archive and the organization in agreeing to be the focus of academic research. While the research of the kind conducted by Smith and Simeone (2017) is possible using published sources and archival records, without the explicit agreement of the archive in question allowing researchers to examine all records, it can be difficult to see exactly how an organization is making use of their archive. Likewise, access would be necessary to fulfil the research agenda discussed by Van Lent and Smith (2019) in their study of the process that affects a manager's sense-making.

In addition to existing relationships that would make the research more likely to be permitted, business historians have developed methodologies and techniques for conducting research in corporate archives. As a result, they are arguably best placed to judge how organizations are using its archives, the rigour with which historical accuracy is pursued, and whether the approach was appropriate for their planned use. Again, research of this kind would likely require the willingness of the corporate archive in question to open itself and its processes up to scrutiny to show how any archival research was performed; what the criteria are for keeping or destroying records; what was requested and expected of them from the parent organization and what processes are implemented in deciding on how the archive is used. While some of this information is often already available – many archives are open about the criteria they use for judging which records are kept and destroyed – not all corporate archives are going to be willing to expose their processes in such a way, particularly if they might face criticism that could undermine their increasingly precarious existence (Adkins & Benedict, 2011). Nevertheless, archivists might be more willing to be open with business historians with whom they already have relationships, who understand the motivations and constraints of corporate archivists (Green & Lee, 2020) and who have an interest in the continued existence and openness of corporate archives as a key source for their research (Popp & Fellman, 2020).

3.7 Conclusions

This chapter has shown just some of the variety of approaches to incorporating history and historical methods into organization studies since the 'historic turn' was announced to the academic world. While rhetorical history and uses of the past research are potentially promising avenues for business historians whose skillsets would appear to be in demand, it is also clear that there are still differences in the ontological and epistemological understandings of the discipline of business history and those that underpin the approach of scholars engaged in the 'historic turn'. ANTi-history has especially stimulated debates about what history is and what historians do, questioning the value of traditional historical research as a producer of knowledge about the past. At the same time, its call for more scholarship examining the past from a variety of viewpoints potentially offers historians a chance to answer criticisms of this kind, shaping the debate and demonstrating the value of their work. In addition, there are serious practical difficulties in ensuring that collaborations between academics from different disciplines can continue, given the way that careers evolve and leading journals continue to pursue a highly focused and theoretically oriented approach to the selection of articles. Likewise, while HOS research offers opportunities for business historians to contribute, as it is aimed at creating knowledge that is both relevant to historians and organization studies scholars, it also creates challenges for business historians who wish to engage with its agenda, not least either the requirement to be fluent in various disciplines or establish multi-disciplinary academic partnerships and publish in journals outside their discipline that might not be beneficial to their career. It is consequently important for business historians not only to make contributions to these areas of research but also to highlight how it is the skills, methodologies and data used by historians that have enabled these contributions.

Research on corporate archives is also a promising direction for business historians, arguably suffering from fewer caveats than rhetorical history, uses of the past or HOS. Business historians already have the professional connections, experience and methodologies to contribute to understanding how businesses utilize their archives, offering the prospect of highlighting best practices for others to follow when using them for their own research. Business historians have long been interested in preserving and opening corporate archives to wider scrutiny, while also being open about the problems inherent in using them for scholarly research; considering the burgeoning interest in them as sources of data and as a phenomenon to be studied, it is both important and logical for business historians to lead the development of this body of research.

4 Business history in social science journals

Having noted how in especially the field of organization studies that business history has over the last two decades attracted a lot of attention, it is also evident that over the last decade there has been an explosion in the frequency of historically oriented research in mainstream management journals (namely, those that rank 4* on the CABS List and/or feature on the FT50 list). This has encouraged the publication of numerous special issues across various management journals with an overtly historical focus, encouraging the development of a much more cross-disciplinary approach across the social sciences. Although again it has been organization studies scholars who have dominated this outbreak, it has also spread to other areas such as entrepreneurship, strategy and international business. This chapter will serve two core purposes: first, it will survey the special issues and identify different ways in which history has been integrated into business and management fields, and second, we will examine the impact this has had on the ways in which history has evolved from business-historical work to more theoretically oriented historical business and organization studies.

4.1 *Academy of Management Review*, 2016

One of the most fruitful areas in which there has been extensive debate over the extent to which business history and management studies should be combined has been organization studies. As we noted earlier, the first stirrings of this debate had been prompted by Zald (1993), Kieser (1994) and Clark and Rowlinson (2004), highlighting rich possibilities in marrying the two methodologies in order better to understand organizational dynamics. This prompted a forceful debate surrounding the notion that 'history matters' in organization theory (Lippmann & Aldrich, 2014; Rowlinson et al., 2014). A

DOI: 10.4324/9780429449536-4

ground-breaking work by Rowlinson et al. (2014) foregrounded what would become a special forum topic in the *Academy of Management Review* (AMR), offering several research strategies for promoting greater 'dialogue between organisational theory and historical theory'. The Rowlinson et al. paper highlights three distinct dualisms: (1) the dualism of explanation which sees historians concerned with narrative construction, whilst conversely, organization theorists subordinate narrative to analysis; (2) the dualism of evidence, in which historians use verifiable documentary evidence, whereas organization theorists prefer to use constructed data and (3) dualism in temporality, which refers to historians' constructed periodization versus the organization theorists' treatment of time as a chronological constant.

Building on these hypotheses, the 2016 AMR special forum featured numerous articles from scholars interested in the synthesis of organizational history and organization studies. It had three core aims. First, the authors wanted to frame organizational history as a distinct branch of organization studies, 'promoting historical research as a way to enrich the broad endeavour of organization'. Second, the authors claim that if 'history matters' then organization theory needs to move beyond the use of history as context and case study towards a more theoretically engaged understanding of the past. Finally, the introduction highlights how the focus on 'history that matters' in the present produces two important considerations: how rhetorical history can be used as a strategic resource in organizations and how they can engage more with historically significant subjects such as slavery and racism (Godfrey et al., 2016; p. 590).

This call was extended by Vaara and Lamberg (2016; p. 644), who proclaimed that 'historical embeddedness should be taken seriously'. Indeed, here the authors are keen to establish the links between historical embeddedness and strategic processes and practices. In this context, the study refers to historical embeddedness as

> the ways in which strategic processes and practices and our conception of them are embedded in and defined by sociohistorical environments. We argue for a strong emphasis on historical embeddedness: one should not merely place processes and practices in context but also understand their inherent historical nature and construction.

They offer three historical approaches that can help align history and strategy. First, they confirm how realistic history can help better understand strategic processes, illustrating how comparative historical analysis can demonstrate the historical conditions, mechanisms and causality in strategic processes. Second, they demonstrate how interpretivist history can add to our knowledge of historical embeddedness in strategic processes, and how microhistory can specifically provide a better understanding of the construction and enactment of these strategic practices. Third, the paper highlights how poststructuralist history can help elucidate the historical embeddedness of historical discourses. Following Üsdiken and Kipping (2014), this study provides a clear illustration of 'history-in-theory', an important distinction that places history as a core component of the theoretical understanding of strategy, rather than simply providing empirical evidence of context. This critical approach to history marked an important turning point in the placement of history as a driver of theory development, rather than being 'resources in a historian's toolbox'.

Perhaps the most impactful article to feature in the *AMR* special forum was the piece by Maclean et al. (2016; p. 609) in which they conceptualize historical organization studies. As we noted in the last chapter, this school of thought was intended to provide a conceptual lens through which historians and organization scholars can develop a 'closer union' through the pursuit of *dual integrity*. The *AMR* article builds on this framework by offering a typology of four different conceptions of history in organization research: history as evaluating, history as explicating, history as conceptualizing and history as narrating. From this base, Maclean et al. are able to develop five distinct principles of historical organization studies – dual integrity, pluralistic understanding, representational truth, context sensitivity and theoretical fluency. Maclean et al. (2017) also followed this study with another paper which featured in *Business History Review*, claiming that the general marginalization of business history in management and organization studies is largely a result of the failure of historians to engage with organization theory. In order to mitigate this failure, they highlight how the road to greater legitimacy for business historians in business and management schools is by exhibiting 'greater theoretical fluency' that produces theoretically informed discourse and, thus, 'demonstrates the potential of business history to extend theory, generate constructs and elucidate complexities in unfolding relationships, situations, and events' (Maclean et al., 2017; p. 457).

The *AMR* history special forum issue contained two further studies that focussed primarily on memory (and forgetting). The first study by Lippmann and Aldrich (2016; p. 658) focuses on the notion of 'collective memory', defined here as 'shared accounts of the past shaped by historical events that mould individuals' perspectives'. The authors extend this by combining the concept of 'generational units' to demonstrate how, 'by incorporating historical concepts in the study of entrepreneurial dynamics', they can 'offer a framework for understanding how entrepreneurs' historically situated experiences affect them'. This study provided fertile ground for understanding how generational units of entrepreneurs emerge and under what conditions. The study by Mena et al. (2016) questions why and how serious cases of corporate irresponsibility can be collectively forgotten. Whilst this study is not overtly connected to historical organization studies, it provides a valuable illustration of how 'forgetting work' can have profound positive and negative consequences for the firm, stakeholders and society. Perhaps most novel here is how the past can be constructed and manipulated by organizations to achieve particular aims and objectives (in this case, the 'forgetting' of, and subsequent disassociation from, scandal). Similarly, the article by Schrempf-Stirling et al. (2016) considers how corporate managers navigate the tricky path of responding to criticisms levelled at practices conducted, and/or decisions made, by previous generations of management. The authors demonstrate how the negative impact on organizational legitimacy can be tempered by reconstructing the past narratives in order to pass on a more legitimate corporate identity to the next generation of corporate managers. The model they offer provides different pathways for how a firm will respond if accused of a historic crime or is associated with a historic scandal.

As a collection of studies, the *AMR* special issue was prominent in establishing the connection between the historian's craft and organization studies, thereby encouraging scholars of organization to look beyond history as simply a 'repository of facts from the past for testing theory' and, thus, creating the new sub-field of organizational history (Godfrey et al., 2016; p. 602).

4.2 *Organization Studies*, 2018

The *AMR* special issue sparked the development of a corpus of research focused on establishing how history can be considered amongst the malleable strategic resources available to company executives. Building on this framework, a special issue of *Organization Studies* featured several articles that demonstrate how the past can be used to shape 'organizational identity, strategy and power'. The authors also demonstrate how this 'contributes to our understanding of the socially embedded character of history in organizations by accounting for the role of materiality, intertextuality, competing narratives, practices, and audiences in how the past is used'. What is novel in the 'uses of the past' approach, as highlighted throughout this special issue, is the emphasis on

> the malleability of interpretations of the past, but also their rela-
> tionship to how organizational actors experience the present and
> set expectations for the future. The past thus is understood as a
> source of social symbolic resources available for a wide variety of
> creative uses.
>
> (Wadhwani et al., 2018; p. 1663)

The introduction to the special issue identifies a crucial distinction be-tween how history has been used by management scholars in contrast to how it is classically used by traditional historians. Specifically, it outlines how historians are interested in context and causality and in-vestigating 'the broader contexts in which historical representations organize actors, their interests, and their struggles'. Conversely, man-agement scholars are more concerned with what they refer to as the 'micro-foundational processes and temporal structures by which his-tory is used in organizations', including 'the types of artefacts used to recall the past and the processes by which organizations recover, use, and forget their past, research that is seen as particularly closely aligned with social memory studies and process research on organ-izations' (Wadhwani et al., 2018; p. 1665). The important distinction here is the difference between the, at times interchangeable, use of the phrases the 'past' and 'history'. As we saw in the last chapter, uses of the past research links to the understanding of history as something that is performed in the present and is separate from the past, with the past seen as the chronological events that have happened prior to the present, independent of our knowledge of them or interpretation of their meaning. In this interpretation, 'the performance of history is integral to how any actor navigates their world and academic history emerges only secondarily,' with the research focusing on how these actors interpret and perform history (Wadhwani et al., 2018; p. 1667). This enables us to see history as 'performative', namely, an 'ongoing set of practices through which the past is used to help actors make sense of the present and imagine the future' (Wadhwani et al., 2018; p. 1667). Through this lens, we see history developing a more practical relevance reinforcing how history can be produced, used and influen-tial in contemporary organizational settings.

Wadhwani et al. (2018; p. 1667) move onto address how organiza-tions use history. Here, they demonstrate how history has been used to forge identities, consolidate social memory, set strategic direction, understand entrepreneurial opportunities, redefine market categories, shape understanding of products, establish new industries, forge social movements, define generational experiences and manage perceptions of change. The articles that feature in the special issue extend and build on these core contributions of history in organizations studies, focusing on three ways that the organizations use and manage the past: for corporate identity and identification, to manage strategic change and the processes they use to control the historical narrative.

The first two articles to feature in the special issue both provide fresh insights into how history can help forge identities and, in turn, identification of companies and clusters. The paper by Basque and Langley (2018) offers five examples of how executives in the present spoke through the founder. This is what they term 'founder ventriloquism' (Basque & Langley, 2018; p. 1703), enabling the company to 'articulate, stretch, preserve or refresh expressions of organizational identity' (Wadhwani et al., 2018; p. 1668). Basque and Langley (2018) note that as the temporal distance from the life of the founder increases, the use of the founder as a resource changes, with early invocations of the founder making heavy use of his words and doctrine, while later evocations become more abstract and focus on the founder's 'vision' without using the founder's own words to explain what that vision was. The founder is consequently a useful historical resource for early and contemporary managers but must be used differently based on the temporal distance.

The paper by Oertel and Thommes (2018) demonstrates how history is used in the process of self-representation in their study of twelve watchmakers in Germany and their differing use of firm-level and field-level historical resources for identification based on the age of the firm. As the editorial to the special issue illustrates, these two papers both examine the identity work of organizations from differing historical standpoints. Whereas Basque and Langley (2018) demonstrate 'the malleability of a single source of history over time', the study by Oertel and Thommes (2018) 'illustrates how history can also be a multi-level resource that can be constructed from historical resources that exist at the individual (founder), organizational, and field (or regional) level of analysis' (Wadhwani et al., 2018; p. 1669).

The next two papers in the special issue focus on the process of strategic organizational change management and develop the concept of rhetorical history identifying history as a malleable strategic resource. The paper by Maclean et al. (2018) introduces *intertextuality* as a form of historical rhetoric used by Procter & Gamble (P&G) to transform the company from a multinational to a global enterprise. They demonstrate how P&G mythologized certain elements of the firm's past and used these myths strategically in numerous company-produced texts to facilitate change, while simultaneously projecting an image of adhering to P&G's historical principles and values. This allowed managers to portray the strategic changes that took P&G from a decentralized, multinational organization where divisions were run as separate businesses to a more globally integrated organization that invested more in advertising, R&D and plant, focusing on cost reduction and maximizing shareholder returns as one 'longstanding storyline of having *the character to do the right thing*' (Maclean et al., 2018; p. 1742). The paper by Blagoev et al. (2018) analyses the process of digitization of physical artefacts in the British museum and illustrates how these physical objects are more than mere 'passive carriers of experience which actors can draw upon' (Blagoev et al., 2018; p. 1758) but actively mould or shape processes of organizational remembering, enabling and constraining the potential for action in the present. Blagoev et al. (2018) do not argue that this was a case of path dependence as actors could choose new directions or reimagine old technologies, instead arguing that this was only possible through the affordances of material objects from the past as they enable or constrain the potential for action in the present.

The final two papers to feature in the special issue provide insights into the idea that history can reinforce notions of organizational power. Lubinski (2018) shows in her study of German business attempts to build affiliations in Colonial India how organizational historical claims are co-created by the organization and the audiences that it is appealing to, often in response to existing ones. While the shape of these narratives is also affected by the context of its creation and method of dissemination, for organizations that operate in multiple nations and contexts 'rhetorical directions' (Lubinski, 2018; p. 1802) can occur when audiences interpret the same narrative in differing and opposing ways. Finally, the paper by Cailluet et al. (2018) demonstrates how the company's ability to manage history as a competitive resource can be limited by the fact that the founder stories that are used strategically and perpetuated by organizations are also adapted and used by external actors, particularly when they are based on figures with a public profile as is the case in this study. While organizations can try to control the historical resources that narratives are based around, such as the archives or historical artefacts, they cannot prevent external organizations from also using the same resources. This limits what an organizational narrative can say as the

presentation of the figure or event must be in line with public perceptions of these figures.

4.3 *Journal of Business Ethics*, 2020

The 2020 special issue of the *Journal of Business Ethics* was specifically
aimed at expanding on the ideas of Schrempf-Sterling et al. (2016),
who introduced the concept of historic corporate social responsibility (HCSR) as a means of addressing questions of responsibility and
accountability for actions taken in the distant past. Schrempf-Sterling
et al. (2016) posit that two key factors determine the effect of historical
misdeeds on present-day corporate legitimacy: *corporate engagement,*
or the ways in which an organization decides to engage with the criticism and the *claim legitimacy* of the narrative being presented which
considers the institutional pressures on the company at the time of
the alleged misdeeds, the magnitude and durability of the harm and
the plausibility of the narrative that affects how receptive audiences
are to the narrative (Schrempf-Sterling et al., 2016; pp. 705–708). The
interplay between these two concepts affects how the past of an organization might affect its contemporary legitimacy, increasing or
decreasing the perceived legitimacy of an organization.

The first article of the special issue introduces three ways that
HCSR has, so far, been researched: the past-of-CSR; the past-in-CSR
and the past-as-CSR (Phillips et al., 2020). The past-of-CSR focuses
on a 'more comprehensive understanding of CSR thought and practice' through the application of historical methods to 'engender critical reflection on the power structures and sedimented relations in
which historical and contemporary patterns of CSR are embedded'
(Phillips et al., 2020; p. 204). The past-in-CSR draws from HOS (see
Chapter 3.4) and focuses on the 'potential for empirical historical research to exposit, substantiate, and even challenge CSR concepts and
theories' (Phillips et al., 2020; p. 206). The past-as-CSR views history
as a mix of an objective past that is interpreted by contemporary actors, with their own interests and viewpoints connected to the present
(Phillips et al., 2020). Conceptualized in this way, history can lead to a
conflict of narratives when new evidence about the past emerges or as
contemporary morals and values change, each providing challenges to
an organization's legitimacy.

Hielscher and Husted (2020) provide an example of the past-of-CSR,
drawing on secondary sources and existing historical research to present the history of medieval miners' guilds in Germany. They show that
what they term as 'the proto-CSR' of the miners' guilds involved a

process of experimentation and adaptation to address changing socio-economic problems. This study also has relevance for how we assess CSR programs today in emerging markets, given that the experimental efforts of these guilds show how CSR programs do not come fully formed and capable of dealing with the social problems facing workers, an issue to consider when judging CSR efforts. The article by Smith and Johns (2020) is another example of the past-in-CSR, exploring the creation and disappearance of the market category of 'free-grown sugar' between the eighteenth and nineteenth centuries, using a mix of primary and secondary sources. They show that the anti-slavery movement of the late eighteenth century stimulated demand for sugar grown without the use of slave labour, a demand that faded following Britain's banning of slavery within the Empire. Through this historical narrative, Smith and Johns (2020) call into question the met-anarrative of ethical progress – that each generation of consumers is more ethical than the last – that is common in the literature on consumer ethics. Additionally, their use of historical methods and both primary and secondary sources shows the potential contribution that history can make to the study of CSR through re-evaluating unquestioned historical narratives.

The remaining two articles are an example of the past-as-CSR, with Coraiola and Derry (2020) focusing on the historical misdeeds of the US tobacco industry, while Van Lent and Smith (2020) look at how HBC manages its past. Coraiola and Derry utilize primary sources to show how the US tobacco industry conspired to hide their knowledge of the dangers of tobacco usage, categorizing these methods into two groups: 'collusive forgetting' and 'collaborative remembering' (Coraiola & Derry, 2020; p. 239). Ironically, acts of 'collusive forgetting', triggered by industry irresponsibility, also prompted acts of collusive remembering as there was a 'fear of litigation [which] put pressure on the organisations not to forget the past and preserve mnemonic assets that would give them an edge in court' (Coraiola & Derry, 2020; p. 247). This study shows the contribution that historical sources and methods can make to the study of CSR, taking the study of organizational memory beyond the study of a single organization to an industry as a whole as well as highlighting the 'layered process' (Coraiola & Derry, 2020; p. 248) which 'transfers the burden of past irresponsible decisions onto future generations of managers' (Coraiola & Derry, 2020; pp. 247–248). Van Lent and Smith (2020) also utilize a longitudinal study to document HBC's CSR strategy in relation to its historical misdeeds over time. This study shows how HBC's approach to its history was affected by its low engagement strategy in the past, as these engagement strategies become embedded in organizational practice, affecting efforts to move to a high engagement strategy and shaping HBC's later reinterpretations of its history. These findings add complexity to Schrempf-Sterling et al.'s (2016) conceptualization of corporate engagement as either high or low by considering how previous strategies become embedded in the organization and continue to affect an organization's view of its history.

This special issue shows the potential contributions that historical approaches can make to the study of CSR, generating new insights, adding complexity to the existing theory and questioning existing beliefs that have directed earlier research. What is notable about these articles is the use of both primary and secondary sources as data, something that is common practice for business historians but is a new approach for CSR scholars. The use of primary sources shows how historical methods and sources can generate theoretical insights that are applicable to understanding contemporary organizational CSR strategies, while the use of secondary sources and existing historical research demonstrates how existing historical analysis can be a valuable data source for research on CSR. Additionally, historical methods that allow for analysis of CSR over time add complexity to existing theory, with the historical act of periodizing, rather than conceptualizing time linearly, helping to contextualize the findings. As Phillips et al. (2020; p. 204) argue, HCSR is still an emerging body of literature and will need to overcome differences in how the past is understood as well as the challenges of meeting the standards expected of historical research. At the same time, it is clear from these examples that historical methods and sources can contribute to evaluating HCSR strategies and are potentially an area to which business historians can contribute, given their focus on how businesses evolve in context.

4.4 Conclusions

In summarizing what these special issues have achieved, it is clear that there are numerous ways in which they demonstrate the role of history in management and organization studies. In many ways, of course, they also reveal some of the core differences between classical or traditional business histories and contemporary approaches to historical organization studies. Specifically, business history is focused on looking back and producing positivist, empirical and, in some cases, biographical and narrative accounts of the past. By this, we mean it examines history by contextualizing and examining causation and consequence/outcomes of events and periods in the history of businesses, industries, entrepreneurs and managers. Conversely, the special issues covered in this section are forward looking, using the past to enable us to comprehend the present and predict the future and offering practical solutions and managerial implications that demonstrate how the past can be used by business and industry leaders purposefully to improve a company's performance. The past, in this context, can also be used to challenge stigma, enhance legitimacy, develop identities and organizational culture, values and ethics, highlighting how the past is a malleable strategic resource that company executives can draw upon to curate and manage their history. A major contribution of these studies is that they maintain contemporary relevance and produce findings that can be used and implemented by executives. In this way, history has found a niche and contribution that enables it to align with the purpose of the business school, supporting the development of the next generation of business leaders.

5 Business history, international business and strategy scholarship

It is clear from what has been covered in previous chapters that the use of historical accounts and historical methods has become a significant concern in several social science disciplines, signifying how to some extent business history and mainstream business and management scholarship are being woven together. Of course, the rich possibilities in this intertwining had been recognized much earlier as a direct result of Chandler's seminal work in *Strategy and Structure* (1962). Indeed, Chandler has been labelled the 'Founder of Strategy' (Whittington, 2008; p. 267), and he was clearly influential in the development of areas associated with dynamic capabilities and organizational evolution. While as we noted in Chapter 2 much of this impetus was lost between the 1970s and 1990s, resulting in business history failing to accommodate the seminal developments in strategic management, international business (IB) and other social sciences, more recently there has been considerable interest in harnessing historical research to enhance these disciplines. This trend was first summarized by Wadhwani and Jones (2016; p. 1), who were primarily concerned with reforging the links between business history and the study of strategy by offering 'three models of historical change – evolutionary, dialectical, and constitutive – which can be used to extend theory and deepen research about the origins, context, and micro-foundations of dynamic capabilities'. Perchard et al. (2017) have also attempted to develop an effective bridging mechanism between historical research and disciplines such as strategy, international business and entrepreneurship, noting especially how, following organization studies' increased concern with the 'historic turn', scholars in these fields were producing research that laid important and fruitful foundations for further collaborations with business historians. Although the volume of articles generated might be regarded as marginal, and just as with organization studies there are methodological issues still to be tackled, several key scholars

DOI: 10.4324/9780429449536-5

have made in-roads in the main IB journals (Acemoglu et al., 2001; Kedia & Bigili, 2015; Buckley & Pérez, 2016; de Silva Lopes et al., 2019), demonstrating the enormous potential in this type of research. Similarly, strategy scholars have responded energetically to Whittington's (2008; p. 267) plea 'to reassert the lost Chandlerian tradition of rich and intimate engagement with managerial practice'. Although we are still some way from creating the kind of 'dual integrity' which the HOS school expect, the dialogue is exciting and potentially rewarding for all disciplines, building an optimism that could well result in greater clarity on issues such as methodology and integration.

5.1 International business

As we noted in Section 2.2, Wilkins (1970, 1974) had pioneered the historical study of IB, and later, she succeeded in engaging economists in a debate about the concept of free-standing companies that she had coined (1988; Casson, 1994). At the same time, as Jones (2021) rightly observes, the case for using history in IB has featured sporadically in the literature, and more recently there have been calls for greater inter-disciplinarity in order to achieve both methodological and theoretical advancement. For example, even if the explication of history specifically as having a role is limited, Shenkar (2021) emphasizes the value obtained through studying culture in IB through a 'humanities' lens. Jones (2021; p. 83) also argues that IB scholarship has followed a sort of 'intellectual path dependency', one which is far too rational and faceless to provide more nuanced meaning for global business and its contexts. Given IB's preoccupation with economics and quantitative methods, which fail to address the contextual realities of global business today, this has played out in both the limitations to methodological approaches adopted and a pursuit of narrow perspectives, more so than in other management disciplines. This brings us back to the seminal work of Pettigrew (1985) on contextualization because as Jones (2021; p. 85) argues business history's principal contributions to IB could well be to act 'as a source for contextual intelligence'. Buckley (2020) had also earlier argued for a greater understanding of 'time' in IB research, highlighting how leading IB scholars were convinced that adding a historical dimension to the discipline would be beneficial.

The literature on a 'historic turn' in IB is largely scattered across journals and special issues, sometimes hiding in less obvious publications that have been carved out for specific historical case studies. This in itself demonstrates something significant about the globalized world of business and the development of multinationals (Acemoglu et al., 2001; Kedia & Bigili, 2015; Buckley & Pérez, 2016). As a result, some scholars have lamented the lack of 'cross-fertilization' between IB and historical research (Kobrak et al., 2018). Kobrak et al. (2018) also argue that while some useful studies exist, they speak only to business history audiences, resulting in what they call the 'echo chamber effect' that inhibits a meaningful conversation between the disciplines. The key to a resolution to this 'echo chamber effect' is much greater use of history by IB scholars, leading to an integration process that can be of mutual benefit.

A crucial debate in many IB journals is an evaluation of issues that pertain to business history and history in general, namely, the argument that the past is 'not a simplified version of the present' (de Silva Lopes et al., 2019; p. 1338). This is confirmed by a wealth of historical cases which exemplify organizational diversity in IB. For example, Peng et al. (2017) and Pant and Ramachandran (2017) use history to explore important shifts across institutions, identity and culture, highlighting patterns and change-over-time in IB. Historical accounts and cases also provide the opportunity to return to well-established theories and offer both supportive, even alternative, examples for a theoretical testing ground. This approach can be seen in a recent study by de Silva Lopes et al. (2019) which uses historical research to challenge aspects of the theory of internalization. The authors demonstrate how the direction of knowledge flow and the trajectory of internalization are misleading and inaccurate because it focuses on the home country segment of the multinational enterprise (MNE) as the initiator of internalization. This study is important because it demonstrates the validity of arguments for applying history in practice. In addition, the formulation and direction of strategy in IB has received some attention, Jones and Khanna (2006) arguing that strategic choice and decision-making are governed by past strategic choices, decisions and, thus, history. This anticipated what the advocates of rhetorical history and uses of the past scholars have argued, illustrating how historical accounts and the evaluation of strategic paths can prove useful to current IB research.

While it is clear that the interaction between business historians and IB scholars is improving, some methodological challenges still need to be overcome. Given that IB has been dominated by economic and quantitative methodologies and historical research tends to focus on qualitative perspectives, there could well be a fundamental challenge to fusing the disciplines. As Jones (2021) identified, the restrictions placed on IB methodologies over time have provided the most significant barriers to integration. Buckley and Casson (2021) also noted that an overreliance on opaque statistical analysis has been one of the core weaknesses of recent IB work, a point supported by Jones (2021). These methodological barriers could well obstruct the way business historians approach and present data, which can appear significantly different in IB journals. While adaptations can be learned, it is important not to devalue the sources and methods in doing so. Reflexivity in understanding archival data is paramount and perhaps some time needs to be spent in explaining uses of history and justifications for sources to an IB audience.

In bringing reflexivity and contextualization into the analysis, historians can help provide a deeper perspective to understanding how over time units of analysis can face characteristic changes, whether it be in a network, multinational, formal institution or small firm. While there is inherent value in the exploration of these 'units', it is essential to understand the context in which change occurs. Similarly, in terms of context, one cannot project a modern lens of understanding on the past; the contextual differences, even if subtle, need to be addressed and explored. Scholars from both business history and IB need to be aware of the dangers of transplanting modern ideas and theories onto historical cases without properly acknowledging or vetting key contextual differences that might impact on outcomes or processes. Of course, this is not to say that qualitative research in IB is less substantive because it is recognized that there are distinct benefits to extending the qualitative approach (Welch & Piekarri, 2017). Jones and Khanna (2006) also propose that a 'micro-qualitative approach' would have substantial value if offering unique case perspectives for the study of internationalization, an oft-contested subject since the development of the 'stages' model (Johanson & Vahlne, 1977). Within their study, Jones and Khanna re-emphasize the value of micro-qualitative studies that can provide us with variegated examples of paths to internationalization, operating modes and multinational identity. This related back to what Morck and Yeung (2007) suggested as 'a shift from breadth to depth' in IB. Building on this proposal, Morck and Yeung (2007) commented on the usefulness of historical data analysis, arguing that IB is one of the core areas of business and management that can benefit from a historical approach. Buckley (2016) supported this claim, arguing that careful use of historical records could enrich our understanding of the internationalization process, thereby enabling the development of frameworks that are more inclusive of variations in both type and contexts that are essential to a more nuanced understanding of the global scene. This links with Suddaby and Foster's (2017) understanding of history-as-sense-making, in that multiple perspectives allow us to forge a more holistic perspective on theories of internationalization and typologies of IB actors.

In reading the select range of core IB journals, several themes can be identified where historical methods and the use of historical accounts and sources could provide further illumination and deepen theoretical perspectives. This is well illustrated by de Silva Lopes et al. (2019), in providing a broader interpretation of theories such as that of internalization when examining the breadth of historical cases. Alongside factors which comprise some of the well-worn theoretical models in IB (such as the OLI paradigm), strategies for internationalization, in general, offer up a diverse kaleidoscope of perspectives when examined through a historical lens. Certainly, arguments for non-linear internationalization (Dominguez & Mayrhofer, 2017) would be reinforced through a study of historical cases.

Buckley and Casson (2021) recently found that the research agenda evolving within the context of *IB Review* shows a move towards assessing MNEs in their respective environs and related responses. Given the caveat we have just noted in relation to contextual intricacies and differences, it is clear that historical accounts and perspectives would be exceptionally useful. Certainly, studies such as Minefee and Bucheli (2021), Aldous and Conroy (2021), Lubinski and Wadhwani (2020) and Decker (2018) add considerable value to perspectives on MNE responses to their environment, particularly in emerging economies. For example, Aldous and Conroy (2021) provide important insights into MNE responses to extreme shifts in specific institutional environments, using the case of British MNEs against the backdrop of Indian independence, producing important observations that add to our understanding of global business in times of institutional flux. In addition, their work provides further justification of the need to understand change over time and the importance of temporality in IB (Bucheli et al., 2019).

In a similar vein, Minefee and Bucheli (2021) use archival data to explore Royal Dutch Shell's strategies and decision-making in South Africa during the apartheid regime. They argue that the use of archival sources alongside access to former company executives 'provide us with a unique window to study the MNE's strategies by zooming in and out between actors' strategies within local contexts, as well as the larger global context' (Minefee & Bucheli, 2021; p. 2). Furthermore, MNE responses need to be viewed through the perspective of 'time' and evaluated in relation to potential path dependency. Path dependency, path creation and path-breaking are all concepts acknowledged within IB that could benefit from greater historical understanding, particularly with respect to how context shapes behaviour, decision-making and the strategic trajectories of global firms (Jones & Khanna, 2006).

Another area ripe for research is one that focuses on the intersections between levels. The micro- and macro-layers of IB are often examined in isolation, whereas authors such as Verbeke and Kano (2015) reveal the interaction between layers is crucial to broadening our understanding of global business, but only with an effective incorporation of history. The evolving literature in IB consequently demonstrates that there are a number of additional research avenues present in IB scholarship which provide opportunities for historians. Alongside what has already been mentioned, one might add foreign direct investment decisions, merger and acquisition processes, organizational learning, the evolution of global business networks, longevity in firms (particularly family firms), international entrepreneurship and growth and change in emerging markets. The landscape looks promising for further inter-disciplinarity and a move away from restrictive and tired methodologies.

5.2 Strategic management

What we have just noted about IB can be replicated with regard to strategic management, as strategy scholars have now started to respond to Whittington's plea quoted earlier (see Section 4.3). Of course, business historians have been writing about strategy for many years (Jeremy, 2002), building on Chandlerian insights to provide stronger links between agents and context. On the other hand, as Pettigrew et al. (2002; p. 13) have noted, 'the interaction between business history and business strategy research has been minimal' in spite of their mutual interest in the processes of change. As we saw in Chapter 2, Pettigrew (1985) had also pioneered the application of 'contextualization' to the study of business, arguing later that: 'History matters. But history is not just events and chronology; it is carried forward in the human consciousness. The past is alive in the present and may be shaping the emerging future' (Pettigrew et al., 2002; p. 700). However, even though leading strategy scholars such as Whittington and Mayer (2000) accepted the validity of incorporating longitudinal studies into their research, as we noted in Chapter 2 little recognition of the value inherent in Pettigrew's work was evident; indeed, there is barely a mention of this research in the expanding business history literature, including the work by Wadhwani and Jones (2016) and Perchard et al. (2017). Similarly, with the exception of Scranton's recent work (2019, 2020), the provocative work of Chia and Holt (2009) on 'strategy without design' has yet to make any impact on the way that business historians assess the origins of strategic decisions, highlighting the gulf that has emerged between the disciplines.

Recently, however, distinct signs of hope have emerged, with leading journals offering new opportunities to analyse how that gulf can be bridged. Of course, as we noted in Section 3.3, several leading social scientists had already contributed significantly to the debate about how firms used their history to improve performance, publishing in leading journals, including the *Strategic Management Journal* (Sasaki et al., 2019). In 2020, this journal also published a special issue, with an emphasis on history-informed strategy research. As Argyres et al. (2020; p. 343) explain, they wanted to discuss 'how and why history and historical methods can enrich theoretical explanations of strategic phenomena'. Developing some of the core frameworks offered in the *AMR* special issue discussed in Section 4.1, the authors introduce the concept of history-informed strategy research by extending the 'history to theory' and 'history in theory' approaches devised by Kipping and Üsdiken (2014). The strategic emphasis of this special issue placed particular focus on the managerial and practitioner implications which help to delineate the core contributions of the editorial, namely, that they recognize the increasing engagement by firms in their past and how they 'reflect on their identities and use this strategically' (Argyres et al., 2020; p. 343). The guest editors are able to demonstrate an increasing engagement by strategy researchers in historical approaches and methods, highlighting how and why this has taken place. They believe that a core objective of strategy research is to understand sources of a firm's sustained competitive advantage. For this task, they believe that history is well suited to achieve such a core objective, arguing that 'if firms with sustained competitive advantages are outliers, then the study of such outliers requires going beyond approaches that emphasize averages and discourage examination of extreme data points'. More broadly, they argue that historical analysis can be highly useful to strategy research for investigating how the context of contemporary phenomena developed, identifying sources of exogenous variations, developing and testing more informed causal inferences and theories, and more easily supporting analyses of path dependence' (Argyres et al., 2020; p. 344). The special issue consequently demonstrates the capacity of historical research, approaches and methodologies to enable researchers to understand crucial dimensions of long-term firm performance, productivity and profitability. Crucially, this highlights how firms not only make use of their history in decision-making and emergent strategies but also 'how interpretations of the past influence strategy making', underpinning the notion that firms can use their past as 'an endogenous strategic resource that can be proactively managed' (Argyres et al., 2020; p. 345).

Delving further into the special issue editorial, it demonstrates the prospects for historical work to enhance strategy research, confirming that history has a dual value: firstly, historical methodological approaches are positioned as a core 'and powerful' tool that can help 'develop new or modify and test existing theories by allowing access to rich historical data and applying historical conditionality to build and test theory in a context specific manner', and secondly, it is argued that 'history and the use of the past can be incorporated into theoretical models, to enrich theoretical explanations of strategy phenomena, thus becoming an important variable in itself in strategy theories' (Argyres et al., 2020; p. 347). This provides further validation of the ability of historical approaches and methodologies to challenge, confirm and test core theories in strategy. Building on this, the guest editors demonstrate precise dimensions of strategy research to which historical approaches can contribute. By providing contextual and foundational dimensions to the decisions, actions and events of the firm, historical methods can 'provide a critical, interpretivist explanation of their causal relationships can shed light on the determinants and processes that shaped organizational outcomes' (Argyres et al., 2020; p. 347). This enables researchers to understand better the causes of strategic action and account for differences in the performance outcomes of different organizations.

The papers that feature in the special use rich historical data and traditional historical methodologies to develop new frameworks for understanding strategic phenomena. For example, the article by Pillai et al. (2020; p. 372) introduces the concept of 'strategic pivots' which they refer to as costly, risky and irreversible experimentations with unknowable outcomes. The authors identified examples by analyses of company histories of firms in the automobile industry. As Argyres et al. (2020; p. 349) explain, the study provides

> [an] example of history-informed strategy research which combines both the "history to theory" and "history in theory" … it not only uses rich, contextualized historical data to provide a deeper understanding of what distinguishes successful versus unsuccessful early entrants, but it also conceptualizes economic experimentation as a historical learning mechanism that influences the future actions of new entrants.

In this instance, we see history being positioned, both methodologically and theoretically, as object and subject of strategic inquiry, demonstrating clearly how history has been (and can be, perhaps should be) used strategically by firms.

The paper by Suddaby et al. (2020) reinforces the idea that the ability to manage a firm's history is an important dimension of dynamic capabilities, given that this is an important part of the process of implementing change management strategies. According to Argyres et al. (2020; p. 353), the paper demonstrates how managers can use 'history to interpret strategic challenges/opportunities facing the firm, or to inspire and persuade stakeholders to embrace their strategic decisions'. To achieve this, the study provides three cognitive interpretations of history – history as objective fact, history as interpretive rhetoric and history as imaginative future-perfect thinking – demonstrating how they can be used by managers to sense and seize opportunities. Indeed, the authors establish how a manager understands how engagement with the firm's history can improve the ability not only to sense and seize opportunities but also to enact and implement change. Moreover, they confirm how history can also be used to mobilize support and endorsement for strategic change from all important stakeholders (Suddaby et al., 2020; p. 530). By developing a conceptual framework for understanding how history can be used by senior management in change management, the study provides an important addition to the manager's strategic toolkit.

5.3 *Strategic Entrepreneurship Journal*, 2020

It was also in 2020 that the *Strategic Entrepreneurship Journal* commissioned a special issue designed to demonstrate the value of historical reasoning and methodologies in that field of research. The emphasis of this special issue was to show how variations in treatments of time and context shape theoretical claims about entrepreneurial opportunities, action and processes of change. Moreover, the special issue is able to shed light on the value of history in understanding variations in entrepreneurial practices (Wadhwani et al., 2020; p. 3). Most notably, it built on some of the core concepts developed in an earlier paper by Wadhwani and Lubinski (2017) which featured in *Business History Review*, proffering a new theoretical framework for entrepreneurial history. In this article, the authors propose 'the "reinvention" of entrepreneurial history as a research field by developing new pathways for considering entrepreneurial activities over time with the emphasis placed on the *processes* that drive entrepreneurship rather than the individuals or institutions'. New entrepreneurial history, as it is coined, examines the temporal development of entrepreneurial processes and is defined as 'the study of the creative processes that propel economic change' (Wadhwani & Lubinski, 2017; p. 767).

The *SEJ* special issue formalizes many of the processes outlined in the Wadhwani and Lubinski (2017) article by exploring the capacity of historical approaches and methodologies to understand 'context, time, and change more explicitly into entrepreneurship research and theory' (Wadhwani et al., 2020; p. 4). To achieve this, the editorial highlights exactly how history can contribute to the broader filed of strategic entrepreneurship, explaining how a deeper engagement with 'historical consciousness' (Suddaby, 2016) can enhance our understanding of entrepreneurship theory. The paper uses as a point of departure Schumpeterian theory (1947, 1949) about the essential function of history in developing both empirical and theoretical understandings of entrepreneurship. To this end, they define history as the

> interpretation of the past in the present... [which] demonstrates how assumptions about the relationship between the past and present shape our understandings of context and time in entrepreneurship theory, and how these, in turn, shape theoretical claims about the nature of opportunities and the extent of entrepreneurial agency.
>
> (Wadhwani et al., 2020; p. 4)

The editorial provides five historical approaches to entrepreneurship that the special issue articles demonstrate. The first of these is socio-economic history (Ruef, 2020), illustrating the historical transformation of the household and its implications for small entrepreneurs' access to labour (Wadhwani et al., 2020; p. 7). The second historical approach covered is cultural history, with Demil (2020) providing a new perspective on the classification of 'mail order catalogues', using interpretive historical methodologies to demonstrate how and when new industry classifications emerged in France as well as how narratives were constructed to facilitate industry categorization. The third historical approach is microhistory, aligning closely with the earlier work of Wadhwani and Lubinski (2017) as it focuses on the role of context in entrepreneurial processes. In pursuing this, Hollow (2020) produces a micro-historical account of how the entrepreneurial networks of Sir Isaac Holden evolved. Utilizing the extensive correspondence network of Isaac Holden, Hollow (2020; p. 66) is able to make three core contributions that enhance our understanding of entrepreneurial processes:

(a) how networking activities take place through specific communication platforms with their own socio-technical qualities; (b) how entrepreneurs have the capacity to actively shape and co-create the context within which their networking activity takes place; and (c) how entrepreneurial networking activity can take place in conjunction with—or as a result of—networking activity in other social movement.

This study in many ways mirrors the approach and methodologies of Popp and Holt (2013) in utilizing extensive correspondence files to help illustrate entrepreneurial processes. The fourth historical approach is comparative history, Godley and Hamilton (2020; p. 89) demonstrating how 'the historical space of experience explains how entrepreneurs make strategic choices regarding collaboration under conditions of complexity and uncertainty'. To achieve this, they analyse the US and UK poultry industries, identifying core differences in the way British entrepreneurs were more willing to forge strategic partnerships with supermarkets, in contrast to their US counterparts. Wadhwani et al. (2020; p. 10) provide a neat summary of the two main contributions of this study. First, the paper

> establishes the role of collective memory in how entrepreneurs deal with entrepreneurial uncertainty generally, and as a basis for entrepreneurial alliance formation [and] how collective memory serves as a basis for entrepreneurial expectations about what might happen and shapes how entrepreneurial actors draw on the past in making judgmental decisions in the present about those possible futures.

Second, the paper offers a key methodological contribution in terms of how each of the cases from the United Kingdom and the United States 'operationalizes time'. On the one hand, the paper illustrates 'time as structure', while on the other hand, it positions time as 'the space of experience'. The final approach is historical case studies, as illustrated by Toms, Wilson and Wright (2020; p. 105), who provide three historical case studies that examine two sources of innovation, technical and financial, and assess the time-dependent impact on the institutional nature of entrepreneurship, enabling them to 'theorize about the relationship between market innovation and financial intermediation'.

As a collection, the articles in this special issue demonstrate the ability of historical approaches and methodologies to help shed fresh light on the core themes of emergent long-run strategies, the pursuit of entrepreneurial opportunities and the ways in which historical insights can enhance entrepreneurship theory. Above all, it provided further support for what Wadhwani and Lubinski (2017) were advocating in aligning business history with the further elaboration of entrepreneurship as both a concept and practice.

5.4 Conclusions

Just as with the developments in organization studies (see Chapter 3), it is consequently clear that prominent scholars in the fields of IB, strategy and entrepreneurship have made strenuous efforts to incorporate historical methods into their research projects. At the same time, as Perchard et al. (2017; p. 3) note, while superficially it appears that the various literatures would appear to be merging, they acknowledge that there remained a 'disconnect' in the methodologies adopted. Building on the work of Andrews and Burke (2007), they propose the adoption of the 'five Cs of historical thinking' – context, change over time, causality, complexity and contingency – as the basis for a closer alignment in methodologies. This approach is beginning to gather some momentum because Mackenzie et al. (2019) have also demonstrated with regard to their study of the hospitality and tourism industries that applying the Andrews and Burke model can produce a deeper understanding by illustrating the temporal and historical dynamics of the discipline that have to date been ignored. The key issue here is the failure of social scientists to acknowledge adequately historical context and change over time, limiting the understanding of the value of history to their research. However, the fault does not lie entirely with social scientists because business historians have been equally remiss in fully incorporating social science thinking in their research. For example, with specific regard to the dynamic capabilities framework, Wadhwani and Jones (2016) have offered three models of historical change – evolutionary, dialectical and constitutive – but to date there is little evidence that business historians have seized this opportunity to develop the appropriate bridging mechanisms with strategy scholars. Whether this is because of methodological differences or the unwillingness of both disciplines to think about how the challenges can be overcome we shall examine further in Chapter 8, where the principal focus will be on these methodological issues and the opportunities to align business history with the social sciences. Regardless of these challenges, though, it is clear that leading scholars across many disciplines are beginning to think seriously about their resolution and how we can move forward on this process of alignment.

6 Teaching history in business and management schools

When in 2003 Van Fleet and Wren (2005) conducted a survey of AACSB member institutions to gauge the extent to which history was present and taught within undergraduate and postgraduate course curricula, they were to be sadly disappointed with the results. Although by that time many business historians had found solitude in business schools, their teaching focused more on strategy, international business, organization studies and any number of 'mainstream' business subjects, rather than on bespoke business history modules. Recently, Jones (2021; p. 77) has also noted that the drive to 'professionalize management education' has created barriers to the incorporation of historical subjects, with words such as 'employability' acting as an intangible gatekeeper. Similarly, despite the recent tendency of leading management journals to sponsor special issues that have examined ways of justifying the value of history to management leaners, this would appear to have had a marginal impact on curricula across the enormous business school world. At the same time, the impact of COVID-19 and the consequent drive to online learning imposed on universities as a result of lockdowns and deep health concerns has stimulated widespread debate about pedagogy and the nature of management education generally. These issues we shall examine in this chapter, focusing especially on the core values associated with the application of business history to the teaching of business and management and the extent to which these can be applied in practice.

One of the first important questions that must be asked is how history is viewed by non-historians, and in particular how the history of business is viewed by management learners and content 'gatekeepers' at business and management schools. Is the history of business even a strand of history that is considered to be appropriate, or does one naturally think of world wars, nation states and royal lineages when 'history' is discussed? One of the main issues observed is a perceived

DOI: 10.4324/9780429449536-6

disconnect between the past and the present (Wright, 2010) and perhaps an idea that the past is a simpler time, free of the complexities we
observe in today's globalized world (de Silva Lopes et al., 2019). On
the other hand, a number of studies have asserted that not only does
engagement with history improve future managers' ability to perceive
and navigate the present (Van Fleet & Wren, 2005), while more generally it can also have a 'positive impact on the future of management'
(Cummings & Bridgman, 2011; p. 77).

Another important question raised by several scholars is whether
there are weaknesses in management learning which the incorporation
of history could serve to strengthen. For example, Wright (2010; pp.
698–699) suggests that there are certain areas of management learning
that could benefit from the reflexivity afforded through the study of
history, providing management learners and potential future managers with an advantageous foresight based on an understanding of how
events have unfolded in the past. Lamond (2005) also suggests that an
understanding of the historical development of management theory
and practice is essential for comprehending how and why things are
done in the way they are in business today. Of course, there is a correct and incorrect way to teach and use history, and students should
be clear on the uses and 'misuses of the past' before it can be utilized
appropriately in practice.

6.1 History and social sciences

As we have seen in earlier chapters, some topics – organization studies,
entrepreneurship, strategy and international business – have already
benefited from the incorporation of history into classroom activities.
All too frequently the first step in the process of integrating subjects
into management school curricula is establishing a strong presence in
the literature. This, coupled with a curriculum that prioritizes the embedding of research and research methodologies into teaching, provides a window of opportunity to bring the most current theoretical
and methodological advancements into the classroom. At the same
time, it is important to add that history has had a greater impact in
certain 'mainstream' management and business scholarship, while
maintaining a stifled presence in others. For example (see Section 3.4),
we have already noted how the Historical Organizations Studies
school (HOS) is one group that has made significant progress in applying longitudinal perspectives to topics associated with organizational change and organization identity. On the other hand, as Decker
et al. (2020; p. 4) note, the use of history within organization studies

is 'being demoted to ensuring empirical accuracy'. If this is the case, this does not then add value to management learners through a true integration of historical methods and approaches into that discipline. It is consequently clear that even though one can observe the presence of history in management scholarship, it sometimes takes a diminutive role, limiting its ability to carve out a distinct place in management school curricula. Crucially, the incorporation of history into management literature must be encouraged in a way that still respects the methodological complexities of studying history and analysing historical accounts; otherwise, learners will have only a partial understanding of the processes of change that the discipline can bring to the social sciences. This means that history can find a place in curricula, as long as it is fully embedded in research agendas and its methodologies are incorporated into the learning process. Beyond HOS and organization studies, other subjects which have developed a growing use of historical accounts and methodologies include international business (Jones & Khanna, 2006; Verbeke & Kano, 2015; Kobrak et al., 2018; de Silva Lopes et al., 2019), entrepreneurship (Bucheli & Wadhwani, 2014; Wadhwani & Lubinski, 2017) and strategy (Whittington, 2008; Ingram et al., 2012; Kahl et al., 2012; Murmann, 2012; Kluppel, 2018). Other topics which run as strands through degrees, such as ethics and social responsibility, have also benefited from the application of a historical perspective (Warren & Tweedale, 2002; Stutz & Strempf-Stirling, 2019), a point further developed earlier in Chapters 3–5. This means that general management learners will be able to engage in some or all of these topics, as they occupy the main foundational aspects of most business degrees.

6.2 Benefits to learners

History departments have long explored the benefits obtained by their graduates from studying the subject, identifying how a transferable skillset can be developed. This line of justification arises because for parents, students and prospective employers, the wider benefits and skills obtained from history degrees are not always readily apparent. This is an issue tackled by Tennent et al. (2020), who have argued that a knowledgeable understanding of the past, one rooted in the concept of 'historical consciousness', can create critical management leaners by encouraging students to reflect on how the past has shaped the present. Historical consciousness consequently becomes an important way in which management learners can, indeed, learn to learn and become reflexive thinkers. Specifically, a deeper and nuanced understanding of context can aid management learners in numerous ways. For example, within international business teaching, studies of 'evolution' or 'development' are common, especially as it relates to understanding globalization, global value chains and shifts in economic development, particularly from East to West (Jones & Khanna, 2006; Buckley, 2016). The role of history within these contexts, and indeed in creating contexts, would certainly benefit from greater focus and articulation within management curricula. Without these longitudinal and contextual perspectives, it is difficult to comprehend that governments transition, conditions change and thus the global economy is in constant flux, aspects of international business that are currently provided in what can only be regarded as a superficial manner.

Alongside adding contextual depth and reflexivity, historical methods and the use of historical accounts can serve to improve how we teach students to conduct research in the context of their studies. As historical approaches have been touted by several management scholars as a new, less conventional method which can add many significant and intricate layers to how we research, learners can be provided with the opportunity to explore historical accounts through the use of archives, thereby adding another methodological approach and source-base. As we have already noted, Tennent et al. (2020) argue that opening up archives to management learners can aid in the development of 'historical consciousness', a particular mode of understanding that is necessary for developing critical reflexivity. A greater methodological understanding between history and business and management studies, particularly from a source perspective, as Perchard et al. (2017) argue, could potentially unlock complexity in student work and research projects, bringing further rigour in source analysis. Indeed, alongside arguments for a wider acceptance of other methodologies within business history research (Decker et al., 2015), they have the potential to provide students with fascinating alternatives to the standard methods they are typically taught, allowing them to achieve a degree of 'methodological pluralism' at an early stage. Additionally, Bridgman et al. (2016) suggest a move away from the more traditional case method to one that includes a broader, longitudinal perspective on business' role in society. This would have the added value of enhancing the overall credibility of business schools in terms of educating future managers in corporate social responsibility. All of this speaks to the overall benefits of inter-disciplinarity (Teece, 2011), which provides a deeper understanding of all the moving parts within the field, as well as a link between theory and practice, and thus an extended ability in the critical evaluation of context, strategy and decision-making.

6.3 Business history and the future manager

As business and management schools have long had the objective (or purpose) of producing future managers, it is important to address what the study of history provides for the future manager. One of these falls under the strategic 'uses of the past' category in developing a manager's ability to plan, predict and make decisions for the future of their business. It is frequently argued that history provides crucial tools to its students, and for future managers, such tools can be used strategically (Burke & Rau, 2010; Cummings & Bridgman, 2011, 2016). Some have even questioned if a greater appreciation of history could see the death of short-termism because by offering an increase in the historical consciousness of students and managers, this could promote longer-term outlooks (see the Yale blog entry by Scott Miller, 2020). Likewise, Lamond (2005) argues that for managers seeking strategic innovation, an understanding of how the past has informed and still exists in the present is essential for knowing how to move a business forward.

A greater understanding of broader forces and how they might play a role in shaping outcomes for businesses and society would, indeed, create seemingly 'enlightened' managers (Smith, 2007). Indeed, Smith (2007) argues that there are many ways in which history can be utilized by management learners to form better managers, from generating a greater knowledge base to improving societal citizenship overall. Wilson and Thomson (2006; pp. 4–5) were also intent on providing managers (future and practising) with an improved historical perspective on the emergence of their profession, arguing especially that 'management needs to be studied in practice as well as in theory'. The principal supporting reasons behind this view were as management is the key factor of production that provides competitive advantage, it is essential to take a long-term view of its evolution; much of the management literature is primarily concerned with offering instructional lessons on the function, rather than an understanding of its wider role in society and crucially, every organization needs to understand and learn from its own past in order to appreciate fully both its capabilities and weaknesses. This highlights how a historical perspective provides the opportunity to question the profession and the environment in which it operates. Managers ought to become critical of past decisions, essentially questioning why certain decisions were made and potentially improving upon those decisions based on a greater understanding of their origins (Oertel & Thommes, 2015). As Cummings and Bridgman (2011; p. 77) argue, 'students would be more likely to have a positive impact on the future of management if they were more engaged with the history and traditions of management'.

6.4   Why its acceptance has been incremental

While there exists at present a rather fashionable strand of history-based research emerging in some of the top management journals, spearheaded by a number of key scholars (Jones & Khanna, 2006; Suddaby & Foster, 2017; Wadhwani & Lubinski, 2017; de Silva Lopes et al., 2019), the real question is whether this momentum will be sustained. History has lingered in some form in management and business studies for decades; the existence of business history journals, numerous business history conferences and the presence of business historians in business schools are testament to this. Additionally, as we noted in Section 2.2, the inductive methodology of industrial economists such as Penrose (1959) could act as an excellent demonstration of how history can inform theory. On the other hand, while the notion of 'evolution' is certainly present in management school curricula, it is generally not packaged as 'history', other than in a very few business history modules dotted across business schools. In the 2003 survey, Van Fleet and Wren (2005) found that teaching of history in business schools was less present than it had been twenty years earlier. Nearly twenty years on from that survey, one can add with some certainty that although the research community of business historians has grown and is even more diverse, the uptake of explicit historical cases or contextual analyses within business school curricula is still lacking. Indeed, historical methodologies, crucial to the proper use of history, are also generally absent from most research methods modules in both undergraduate and postgraduate teaching.

It is consequently necessary to examine the roadblocks or gatekeepers. Why is there a reluctance to teach history and call it 'history' within a management or business school setting? The first obvious reason is the general absence of those that can teach history. While we have already noted that business historians have taken refuge in management/business schools (primarily because of the collapse of economic history and declining recruitment into history programmes generally), rarely can one detect a critical mass capable of decisively influencing the curricula. Second, as history as a subject is considered to be specialist, and therefore its incorporation is seen as niche without an explicit link to management learner outcomes, business schools have been reluctant to approve dedicated modules. Rightly or wrongly, it has been assumed that the adoption of a history-focussed module would either affect student satisfaction or, if made optional, receive very few subscribers. This would explain why those business historians who have run business schools failed to inject their own discipline into the curricula, given the financial and student experience pressures imposed by university management's desire to extract full value from these faculties.

Linked to this issue is the attitude of employers, and consequently of parents who frequently provide funding for a university education. Increasingly over the last forty years, the attitude to investing in achieving a university degree is associated with employability, with higher education's role to provide a core skillset that can be applied directly in the worlds of practice. Specifically with regard to management education, business schools are charged with the task of generating the next generation of managers and leaders, to a certain extent acting as substitutes for internal training. In addition, given the increased emphasis on applied research and impact that features prominently in the policies of both research funders and government policies, academics' attention has been focused on their normative impact, rather than on any vision associated with intellectual development. This environment has inevitably had a direct impact on the extent to which history can influence business school curricula, especially as the Deans of these institutions would look askance at the diversion of resource into modules or programmes that do not generate adequate income to cover its costs.

6.5 Conclusions: how to integrate into the business school through a stepped approach

Regardless of this distinctly unhelpful environment, it is nevertheless clear that the integration of business history into management education has kaleidoscopic benefits, especially if a stepped approach to such integration is taken. One might argue that module learning outcomes set in a number of subjects across the business school, such as strategy, international business, entrepreneurship and organization studies, could benefit from the organic adoption of historical case studies and methods in their modular learning plans. Especially in scenarios where business historians are teaching such subjects, many will already be undertaking integration of this type as part of a research-led teaching agenda. While the teaching of historical methods is likely to be less common in mainstream business research and analytics modules, as Tennent et al. (2020) argue, navigating the archive, as well as questioning the creation and purpose of collections, can help management learners develop both their historical consciousness and more critical and reflexive learning styles. Indeed, they also suggest that data triangulation arising from working with rich archival data is an important skill for dealing with complex issues. As we also noted in Chapter 1 and Section 5.5, it ought to be possible to utilize the 'five Cs of historical thinking' offered by Andrews and Burke (2007; p. 1), given that they 'provide a remarkably useful tool for helping students at practically any level [to] learn how to formulate and support arguments based on primary sources, as well as to understand and challenge historical interpretations related in secondary sources'.

While the organic integration of historical cases and methods into core business modules is clearly possible, even better would be the creation of bespoke business history modules. There are current examples that have been championed by clusters of business historians within business and management schools across the globe. Friedman and Jones (2012) provide a comprehensive list in their *Guide to Business History Courses Worldwide* although this is likely to have changed in recent years. The most notable examples are those offered by Harvard Business School within the MBA curriculum as well as the extensive range of modules at Copenhagen Business School. Other Business or Management schools which offer explicit business history modules are Henley Business School, Nottingham University Business School, Schulich Business School (York University, Canada) and York Management School (through the Business Humanities module), to name but a very small selection.

A step further than business history modules would be the creation of business history degrees. Importantly, the content of those degrees would certainly determine if the degree belonged in a business school or history department. Most business schools would certainly baulk at the proposal of a traditional 'history degree' being added to their portfolio, for the reasons outlined earlier. Even more likely, if the degree did not align to principles governed by accreditation bodies, such as AACSB's stringent Assurance of Learning requirements, there would be no place for such degrees. That said, a business history degree would bestow significant benefits, including the addition of methodological rigour; assessing the ways in which organizations might *use* history and following the lead given by significant business and management journals that have recently started to feature history-oriented articles.

While certainly not a 'mass market' degree, business history degrees could find their way into a business school's postgraduate portfolios, particularly in schools that have thriving researcher communities in which this degree could be used as a steppingstone to doctoral studies. While the possibility of a business history degree offered by a business school could well be too radical a shift, there is certainly greater acknowledgement of the value history and historical approaches can provide to management curricula and management learners. Indeed, while business historians will continue to thrive in business and management schools across the globe, extolling the values of history in management education whenever they can, it is incumbent on them to make this happen.

7 Business history

Impact?

The aim of this chapter is to provide some insights into the 'third pillar' of this book, namely, the impact business history might make on practice. Specifically, we will elaborate on why business history has failed to make deeper inroads into the mindsets of practitioners and policymakers and offer some practical ideas on how business historians can engage with the world of policy and practice. We hope that this will motivate scholars to think more broadly about the relevance and potential significance of their research, extending its provenance well beyond academic journal publications, which are all recognized as a narrow tool to measure and achieve research impact. The views in this chapter are informed by over a decade of experience of one of the authors in advising UK policymakers and regulators in the financial services sector, alongside another author's considerable experience in business school leadership. Detailed reference to a significant impact case study for the recent REF will also be presented, demonstrating how the close interaction between experienced business historians who have been working for over thirty years to embed business history can directly influence the work of practitioners and policymakers.

Research impact is often seen as an effect academic research has outside academia on various communities of practitioners, regulators, policymakers, managers and society at large. It can broadly be defined as an auditable or recordable occasion of influence arising from research (Haley, 2018). Academics are increasingly expected to achieve success in research and teaching as well as have a positive impact on stakeholders within and outside academia (Sandhu et al., 2019) through engaged scholarship (Van de Ven & Johnson, 2006; Van de Ven, 2007; Aguinis et al., 2013). However, although many management researchers attempt to make an impact on practice, they often fail to do so (Sharma & Bansal, 2020). This phenomenon is widely known as the 'research-practice' gap, which is said to exist because

DOI: 10.4324/9780429449536-7

researchers seek rigour through generalizable and defensible insights, while managers prefer relevant and context-specific, prescriptive advice (Kondrat, 1995; Van de Ven, 2007; Sharma & Bansal, 2020). This relevance gap is considered to be a problem of 'lost in translation', or a knowledge transfer problem, whereby useful knowledge is being created by academics but not finding its way to practitioners. As a result of this tension, only a few scholars consider that their roles and academic identities should include informing the general public discourse (Hoffman, 2016; Haley, et al., 2021). Although the relevance of academic research and teaching to practising managers has been a subject of debate for many years (Bailey & Ford, 1996; Mintzberg, 1996; Starkey & Madan, 2001; Pfeffer & Fong, 2002), the gap between theory and practice and between rigour and relevance remains.

7.1 Misaligned incentives: 'publish or perish'

The nature of scholarly work in business schools prioritizes academic excellence through rigorous scientific research, a process that makes the knowledge generated less relevant to practitioners (Hughes et al., 2011). This theme has been developed by many leading scholars, including Alvesson et al. (2021) who highlight especially how academic research, in general, has become 'roisearch', or rather it is measured on the 'rate of return in staff investment', as opposed to the broader value of the knowledge generated. Social science scholars all too quickly learn how to write for journal editors in order to progress their careers (Aguinis et al., 2013), eschewing the need to generate knowledge that will benefit society. At the same time, as we have noticed several times in this book, the focus of both funding bodies and government policymakers is becoming increasingly concerned with the application of research, placing more emphasis on impact. This theme has been recently developed by MacIntosh et al. (2021), who have outlined in detail how management research especially ought to be channelled much more extensively towards the applied end of the spectrum and make a broader impact than simply filling learned journals. Only slowly are business school leaders waking up to this challenge, as a result of which scholars will struggle to escape from the 'publish or perish' straitjacket.

All too often the key criterion of academic career success and impact is regarded as publications in high-ranking journals (Adler & Harzing, 2009). Other 'exhibits' of academic success include obtaining a grant; receiving a research or teaching award; recruitment by another university (ability to move/relocate to a better job) or being elected to a leadership role and, of course, more top-rated publications (Kraimer et al., 2019). Having noted these aspects of academic careers, at the same time it is clear that the current higher education environment is changing rapidly and in particular through a greater emphasis on: increasing commercialization and competition; reduced government funding and increased costs; more public scrutiny over governance and value-added activities; greater pressure to deliver the skills required to achieve economic and social outcomes; and the increased expectation on academics to do well as well as do good in society (Hudson & Mansfield, 2020). For academics it means focusing too much on the 'publish or perish' career strategy, which often emphasizes 'productivity' over key issues such as creativity, innovation and public engagement. This focus can also result in reduced cognitive and emotional engagement at work, for example, working on multiple projects at the same time with short deadlines, often generating the feeling of not being able to complete all to a sufficiently high standard, resulting in further feelings of anxiety and frustration (Sandhu et al., 2019).

Academic career incentives to focus on publishing in top-tier journals have created a 'winner-takes-all' system in which someone who is a little better receives a disproportionate amount of the benefits available. There are no benefits at all for 'almost' publishing in a top journal, while the benefits of publishing an article in a lower-tier journal diminish rapidly. Indeed, although the norms of 'publish or perish' are clear and publications in top-tier journals and citations of this work are simultaneously considered to be measures of both success *and impact* (Adler & Harzing, 2009), the rejection rates within these journals have been increasing from 70% in the 1970s to 90% and above more recently (Macdonald & Kam, 2007). When assessing academic career success, Phillips (2019; p. 307) has accurately described this current state of play by saying that:

> '*Academic publishing, like professional sports and the music business, is a world of a few highly visible 'stars' whose extreme efforts are linked to their success and whose visibility makes their examples powerful. Their high status ensures many seek to emulate their success, while the system ensures only a few can... [Academic] status is a zero-sum game, and its extreme concentration in a few individuals and a few universities necessarily leads to lower status for most members of the profession and most institutions. The extremely skewed status distribution is a characteristic of academic system. Every academic field is mostly populated by unhappy losers in the publishing*

*status struggle and...there is simply no way to solve this without rad-
ically restructuring the publishing system'.*

This narrow emphasis on publication at the expense of everything else
in the field of management has certainly been echoed in business history research. Historians are rarely involved in policy debates. Moreover, most business historians either do not think they ought to engage
with practitioners or simply do not know whether and how they can
make their research relevant to current practice, and particularly to
policy. Consequently, business history research seems to have failed
to make much of an impact in this area. Although Chandler's work in
the 1960s did have an impact on the consultancy profession, this remains the exception to a rule which extends to a significant proportion
of business history research. What can be done to disrupt this trend?
Some scholars have begun to indicate that potential practical use can
be derived, for example, from the development of historical organizational studies and rhetorical history research (see Sections 3.3 and 3.4),
while others argue that working more closely with firms on projects
such as developing effective use of archives could well be more beneficial to society than publishing articles and monographs.

7.2 Towards more inclusive scholarship
through engagement and impact

As we noted in Section 2.2, while business history research has often
been viewed mainly as commissioned work used in corporate rhetoric,
either to improve organizational image or to be used as a PR tool, more
recently (see Section 3.3), a genre of work has emerged under the theme
of 'rhetorical history' (Suddaby et al., 2010; p. 147) which purports to
explain how 'history [can be regarded] as a source of competitive advantage', or even a precursor for change (Suddaby & Foster, 2017). This
genre has been extensively evaluated in Chapter 3 and in particular the
links it makes between historical research and the way in which management has used this material in the interests of improving competitive advantage. Crucially, rather than viewing history as an objective
variable beyond managerial control that constrains an organization's
ability to adapt, history can be seen as a core managerial competence
from which managers can develop a 'historical consciousness', or a degree of reflexivity about history as an endogenous symbolic resource of
the firm that can shape corporate action. (Suddaby, 2016).

The emergence of this rhetorical history literature could clearly have
provided business history researchers with an enormous opportunity

to influence practitioners. However, it is vital to note that in the concluding sections of almost all the articles linked to this genre, authors emphasize the relevance of their research to the theoretical literature on management and organizational identity, rather than to practical applications. Rarely one would find any mention of the relevance of such research to the world of policy and practice; research engagement is mostly discussed in terms of engagement between business historians and organizational theorists (Rowlinson et al., 2014). Similarly, an examination of one of the Special Issues on 'Narratives and Memory' in *Organization* (2014) reveals that none of the articles actually dedicate any intellectual space to considering the implications of how the research could be applied to practice. Even articles relating to business and banking (Musacchio Adorisio, 2014), including archival and oral-history research on organizational change at Procter & Gamble (Maclean et al., 2014), made no mention of how this research could improve or contribute to the development of future commercial strategies of these organizations. Indeed, the 'impact deficit' in top-tier journals is a trend imitated in almost all other outlets.

Few would disagree that top-tier academic journals are aimed primarily at academics and theory development, rather than at practitioners (Hambrick, 2007; Bartunek & Rynes, 2010; Hughes et al., 2011). Although most top-tier journals invite authors to elaborate on the contributions to practice, in reality 'evidence in the form of successful implementation of the results in practice is not required' (Kieser & Leiner, 2009; pp. 522–523). This approach has raised many concerns about the significance and implications of academic research to practice. For example, there is a widespread perception that editors and reviewers of top-tier journals are not supportive of such sections and that an 'implications for practice' section actually undermines the academic credibility of an article (Bartunek & Rynes, 2010).

In this context, it is consequently clear that such an approach to 'doing' business history research continues to exacerbate the perception of a lack of practical value, function and purpose of business history research. This returns us to a fundamental question: what are business historians good for? The emphasis on theorization in top management and organization studies journals at the expense of everything else seems to exacerbate the lack of confidence and/or motivation of business historians to engage with other stakeholder audiences and contribute to ongoing debates in policy and practice. Either developing fresh theoretical perspectives or even contributing to debates about theoretical concepts is extremely challenging for any historian who has never been educated in social science methodologies. Moreover, even if Suddaby (2016; p. 47) proclaims that 'there has never been a better time to be a business historian', as we have argued in earlier sections it is difficult to match the expectations of management journal editors with what business historians have been trained to produce.

Notwithstanding these challenges, business history researchers can both do well in their careers and do good. More recently, pluralistic criteria for assessing academic career success and impact in academia have started to emerge (Sandhu et al., 2019). Similarly, grant-awarding organizations have underlined an increasing social need for research that engages with broader audiences. For example, there are AACSB's Assessment and Impact conferences; National Science Foundation's broader impacts and the UK's Research Excellence Framework impact case studies (Haley et al., 2021). Bearing this in mind, we will now turn to discuss some examples of meaningful business history research engagement and impact and in so doing contribute to a perceptual change of what makes for impactful business history scholarship.

7.3 A business history impact case study

Business history research can and does have the ability to contribute meaningfully to the development of future commercial and political strategies. Given our earlier notion (see Section 2.1), which sees business history as a window on key aspects of society and human activity, providing a rich, nuanced, empirically based understanding of how business interacts with and influences the world around it, business history scholars can impact the world of policy and practice not only through the use and citation of published work but also through interaction between academics and practitioners. Despite the possible tensions involved in such an interaction, it is fundamental to knowledge creation and transfer (Hughes et al., 2011). A key strength of business history research stems from its ability to put current issues in proper context, something that is often lacking in practitioner and policy debates.

An outstanding example of business history research engagement and impact comes from Prof. Tony Webster and his work with The Co-operative Group. Initially, this stemmed from the collaborative project on the history of The Co-operative Group (Wilson et al., 2013), a book that was used extensively in the Myners Review into the corporate governance of The Co-operative Group. Having been appointed as a Senior Independent Director to The Co-operative Group in December 2013, Lord Paul Myners conducted a comprehensive, independent review of the Group's governance. The report was published in May

2014, providing a set of practical reforms intended to strengthen the Group's ability to recover from the traumatic shocks it had suffered in 2013 and help position it for renewed success. Crucially, by assessing the corporate governance challenges of The Co-operative Group over the span of 150 years presented in Wilson et al. (2013), Myners was provided with a detailed understanding of how the organization had evolved. More recently, Webster's work has also helped a range of key stakeholders, including the Bank of England, to see how the crisis was partly the culmination of the long-term weakening of the organization's institutional and ideological values (Webster et al., 2016a, 2016b. 2017; Webster, 2019; Webster et al., 2020).

While the Myners Review revealed systemic governance weaknesses in board appointment processes, strategic misjudgements and a lack of board member expertise and influence which ultimately led to diminished performance, subsequent reports by an influential economist John Kay and the Ownership Commission (2012) have highlighted that governance problems are certainly not a co-operative monopoly. Kay especially noted that what was happening at The Group was a microcosm of wider issues affecting UK businesses. These observations echoed Webster's insights into The Co-operative Group, given the isolation felt by many members from the senior layers of executive management, while the lay board lacked sufficient expertise to influence strategy (Wilson, 2014).

Beyond this example, it is clear that business history research has a considerable relevance to larger, more general topics of human relationships and behaviour under changing technological circumstances as well as how this affects the structure and power relations in modern society. For example, research-based knowledge about how political culture, social structures and business practices interact over time in different contexts can advance knowledge in the fields of history, social sciences and management. Similarly, historical studies of leadership, and the social and democratic dimension in different political and geographical contexts, have the potential to highlight the importance of good, as well as bad, leadership not only for business itself but more importantly for the development of modern society.

In the United Kingdom, historical research can shed more light on how organizations create and practice values. This is particularly relevant in the current context where recent surveys suggest that society's trust in business, government and some public institutions (for example, the media and political systems) are at a historic low (Edelman Trust Barometer, 2021). The impact of recurring corporate collapses raises questions about the social legitimacy of corporations, prompting further reconsiderations of what constitutes good (even, best) corporate governance practices in the United Kingdom and around the world (Tilba, 2017). The ongoing UK reviews and developments of corporate governance codes (Financial Reporting Council, 2019) and the increasing emphasis on restoring trust in organizations and institutions (Beckmann et al., 2015; British Academy, 2021) place greater emphasis on understanding what underpins values-based leadership. This consequently provides ample opportunities for business historians to connect their research to current policy debates and perhaps even shape future research agendas.

Perhaps the most effective way of communicating, co-creating and disseminating academic research is through Industry Knowledge Networks. There are multiple examples of formal and informal networks, often set up by industry, with the set purpose of providing a means of engagement between different stakeholders such as industry practitioners, academics, regulators, policymakers, NGOs and other stakeholders. These networks create a potentially effective outlet for social interaction. For example, networks in the financial services sector include the Centre for the Study of Financial Innovation (CSFI), UK Sustainable Investment and Finance Association (UKSIF), Pension Investment Academy (PIA), and the Investment Association, to name but a few.

In the context of Design Science's increasing popularity – an approach to science concerned with developing knowledge that provides answers to social problems through collaboration between various stakeholders (Van Aken, 2004) – there is a particularly good example of productive, influential and longstanding knowledge networking embodied in the UK Transparency Taskforce (TTF). This organization is a collaborative, campaigning community dedicated to driving up the levels of transparency in financial services, both in the United Kingdom and across the world. TTF's mission is to promote ongoing reform of the financial sector so that it serves society better, undertaking a broad range of activities to raise awareness of the lack of transparency in financial services, and how through collaboration people can work together to help put things right. There are regular symposiums that bring together academics, practitioners and policymakers in the United Kingdom and elsewhere, while the TTF also submits evidence and responses to government and industry consultations on such topics as financial fraud, the future of regulation and the use of technology, all of which ultimately create better value for consumers.

Through being an Ambassador for this organization for many years, one of the authors of this book was able to disseminate and co-create current governance research and influence both policy and practice, activity which now forms an important part of an impact case study. When it comes to business history, numerous discussions during TTF symposiums highlighted how historical research can be helpful in terms of providing 'intellectual space' when discussing failures and improving culture and corporate practices without blame for what has happened in the past. Rather than indulging in 'banker-bashing' case studies, this work has helped create a safe intellectual platform in which academics and finance professionals can have informed and frank conversations about where the industry has been and where it really is now, with the emphasis on looking forward (TTF, 2020).

Indeed, there are many different ways in which the interaction between business historians and practitioners could be fostered. For example, one can identify a range of avenues, including public lectures, participating in industry round tables and seminars, submissions of evidence and testimonials to parliamentary working groups and policy consultations, memberships of industry advisory boards and taking up parliamentary fellowships as well as doing commissioned research and commercial consultancy. In their examination of the relationship of top-tier journal contributions to management practice and practitioners, Bartunek and Rynes (2010) find that the most common recommendation is for practitioners to be 'more aware' of certain phenomena, given that frequently empirical or theoretical research has provided fresh insights into the issues. Other popular implications for practice included calls to 'conduct training'; engage in 'learning'; (re)design or (re)structure something and change recruitment, selection or hiring procedures. Although many 'implications for practice' sections in theory-driven academic journals are written in a complicated language and lack information about *how* practitioners could apply findings, academic research does still add value and provide useful direction to practitioners in a variety of ways beyond just application.

7.4 Conclusions

Simply to 'be aware' of something or learn to see something in a different light is important because a newly acquired awareness can often result in active, rather than mechanic, processing of taken-for-granted information (Petty & Cacioppo, 1986). A recommendation to 'be more aware of' for managers could consequently be significant in stimulating conscious processing of information and lead to important changes in practices or behaviour (Bartunek & Rynes, 2010). What scholars can also do to help connect their research to current practice is to link the findings of their studies to resolving more generalized problems or changing assumptions as well as provide more information about context. As Bartunek et al. (2006) put it, 'properly conveying context contributes to telling a story', making research more interesting, relevant and impactful. In a highly competitive world, academics, including business historians, need to learn how to 'blow their own trumpet' louder. Meaningful engagement with other stakeholders can and does have the potential to enrich academic careers, job satisfaction and academic research.

8 Conclusions
Whither business history?

Over the last six decades, business history has progressed from being a subject widely regarded as a sub-discipline of economic history into a fully-fledged discipline with its dedicated professional associations and highly regarded journals. Moreover, if the impressive list of special issues reviewed in Chapters 3–5 is to be regarded as evidence, many areas of the social sciences have recently shown a big interest in harvesting the rich crop of business history research that has emerged since the 1970s. The nature of this progress, however, also highlights one of the principal themes of the book, namely, that in terms of our 'three pillars' of research, teaching and practical impact, only the first has flourished globally, while the other two are languishing some way behind. At the same time, regardless of the substantial literature that has been generated on the subject of forging stronger links between these fields, no consensus has emerged about how to reconcile the epistemological and ontological differences between business history and management and organizational sciences (hereafter, MOS). While we share Kipping et al.'s (2016; p. 19) claim that business history 'is in an inventive mood, bursting with multiple futures and paths forward', there remain fundamental issues that have yet to be resolved. Moreover, even though Chandler's *Strategy and Structure* (1962) succeeded in infiltrating both contiguous disciplines and the world of management consulting, this proved to be a false dawn for the emerging discipline; business history might well have secured an established presence in some institutions such as Bocconi, Copenhagen Business School, Glasgow, Harvard, Northumbria, Oslo, Reading and York, but they are very much exceptions to the rule that in terms of teaching and practical impact the discipline is neglected. Crucially, business history is still struggling to form an identity, especially in the broad field of management education where it is marginalized and even dismissed as irrelevant to the development of future or existing managers.

DOI: 10.4324/9780429449536-8

This chapter will be principally concerned with two core issues: re-inforcing our view of business history as an empirically based disci-pline and advocating the most effective methodology to pursue and assessing how best to enhance the status of business history as a dis-cipline, especially in terms of teaching and practical impact. The title 'whither business history' has been deliberately chosen as a play on words because one possible scenario is that the discipline will only be known for its journals and conferences unless effective remedial ac-tion is taken, just as economic history suffered after 1980. Indeed, the parallels with the latter are daunting, in that having been overtaken by a drive to incorporate econometrics into historical analysis, economic history rapidly diminished in importance as a university subject. There are fears that the same will happen to business history if, for example, the historical organization studies (HOS) school of thought comes to dominate or academics in business schools are obliged to publish only in theory-oriented MOS journals. It is consequently essential to con-sider a strategy for the discipline based on the need to enhance its status and especially to extend the successes achieved with regard to the research 'pillar' into teaching and practical impact. A proposal will be offered in Section 8.2 based on past and current experiences, hopefully providing inspiration to those scholars with the ambition and drive to fashion the discipline's future direction.

8.1 Current debates

One of the most consistent features of both business history and some leading MOS journals over the course of the last two decades has been the search for effective ways to align these two areas of research. Whether any of this academic endeavour has proved beneficial to ei-ther remains a deep source of contention, while at the same time, with the exception of work by Tennent et al. (2020), relatively little effort has been devoted to assessing ways in which business history can influence the other two 'pillars' of teaching and practical impact. Decker (2016a; p. 222) has even noted that within business schools there is 'a divergent marketplace for historical research', with business historians vying for intellectual ascendancy with those who write management and organ-izational history (MOH). The *Routledge Companion* series has perpet-uated this split by publishing separate volumes on the two fields, with little or no overlap in authors, methodology or conclusions (McLaren et al., 2015; Wilson et al, 2016). Jones and Zeitlin (2007; p. 3) had also noted this growing divergence, differentiating between those who be-long to professional business history associations and a broader group of MOS scholars who research historical business developments. This highlights a fundamental issue for the first group, in that the divergence exacerbates the challenge associated with building a consensus on epistemological and ontological issues, not to mention the equally challenging aim of establishing a clear identity within academia.

To elaborate further on this issue, we noted in Section 2.1 that just as business history was emerging as a discipline in its own right from the 1970s, Hannah (1983) was highly critical of the preoccupation with single case studies that contributed little to an improved understanding of business and management. Hannah was especially keen to encourage business historians to align more closely with economics, a line further developed by Lee (1990, 1990a) in an equally devastating critique of the discipline's increasing isolation from the social sciences. Of course, industrial economists such as Penrose (1959) had demonstrated effectively how an inductive methodology could provide a way forward for business historians, while Pettigrew's (1985) study of organizational change at ICI offered yet another way of aligning the discipline to innovative developments in strategy. Nevertheless, and especially after Chandler's contributions had been effectively undermined by a wide range of critics, business history would appear to have resisted exhortations to develop a robust methodology that would accommodate the requirements of social scientists. This highlights once again how the work of Chandler marked something of a false start for business history, a position that is still being assessed during the first decades of the twenty-first century.

It is also clear that the divisions that emerged over the last two decades have deepened, with business historians reaffirming their commitment to an empirical approach embedded in archival research and full contextualization, while schools such as the historical organization studies movement or those advocating rhetorical history persist with their social science-oriented approaches. This fragmentation can also be illustrated through the exchange between Taylor et al. (2009) and Toms and Wilson (2010), the latter arguing in favour of an archives-based approach, in contrast to the former's preference for a French philosopher. As we have noted in Chapter 1, we support the use of what Andrews and Burke (2007) describe as the 'five Cs of historical thinking' of context, change over time, causality, complexity and contingency. Similarly, in spite of the criticisms levelled by Hannah (1983), the advocacy of a 'narrative turn' in business history by Popp and Fellman (2016) is highly appropriate to a discipline that is dominated by historians (Álvaro-Moya & Donzé, 2016). Although some business historians, and especially those employed in business schools, have pursued 'a restless search for legitimacy' by seeking to align business history and MOS, the latter 'are fields hostile to or uncomprehending of historical methods' (Popp & Fellman, 2016; p. 1242). Van Lent and Durepos (2019a; pp. 1751–1752) have also differentiated between the 'history as theory' pursued by MOS scholars and the 'history as method' preferred by historians. This highlights the ontological and epistemological differences that distinguish the two fields (Suddaby, 2016) because whereas management scholars emphasize theory and are critical of pure empiricism, historians focus on empirical data and are highly sceptical of theory (Van Lent & Durepos, 2019a; pp. 1751–1752). In other words, as Durepos and Mills (2012) argue, in order to determine what value history can add to knowledge of organizations, one must be clear about what history exactly is and how it should be written.

Of course, there have been further attempts to bridge this gulf, Suddaby (2016) arguing that both historians and social scientists need to relax their disciplinary commitment to specific ontological and epistemological prescriptions. There have also been special issues in *Management and Organizational History* (edited by Mills et al., 2016), *Business History Review* (edited by Friedman & Jones, 2017) and *Business History* (edited by Decker et al., 2018), all of which offered creative solutions to this conundrum. As Friedman and Jones (2017; p. 455) concluded, however, apart from advocating an extension of business history research to cover areas other than the United States, Western Europe and Japan, 'The Editors do not believe there is a single methodological path going forward. We do believe it is time to engage explicitly with alternative methodologies and to discuss their relative merits and shortcomings'.

In this context, one might also consider the case made by de Jong and Higgins (2015) in another Special Issue of *Business History* supporting the development of what they termed 'New Business History'. Specifically, de Jong and Higgins (2015; pp. 1–2)

> advocate that the current typical approach in business history – dominantly case study analysis – maintains its prominent position, but the purpose and relevance of this type of research in the scientific method for business history is made more explicit. Moreover, we propose the application of additional empirical approaches in business history, which specifically aim to develop theory and test hypotheses.

This idea was further developed in one of the Special Issue articles by de Jong et al. (2015; p. 59), recommending 'the embedding of descriptive case study analysis in a methodological framework encouraging the development and testing of hypotheses'. Above all, as the contribution by Decker et al. (2015; p. 222) outlined, it was essential to acknowledge the 'plurality of methods' that have emerged across business history, a point reinforced by other articles in this volume by Whittle and Wilson (2015) on the application of ethnomethodology to study the practical reasoning procedures used for generating and interpreting historical evidence or that by Higgins et al. (2015) which subjects archival and financial data to econometric testing. As we noted earlier, this call for 'plurality' was also repeated in the *Business History Review* Special Issue on 'Debating methodology in business history' (2017). At no stage, however, did these Special Issues offer a resolution to the fundamental challenges already outlined with regard to the epistemological and ontological differences between historical and social science research. As such, while one can support their aim to encourage debate about these issues, they highlight the continued divergence that will persist.

This accurately summarizes the state of the current debate, in that little consensus has emerged from the extensive range of research analysed in this book. Of far greater significance is the work of Popp and Fellman (2016; p. 1242), who strongly advocate 'a re-engagement with the broad field of historical studies [for business historians], where numerous analytical tools, methods, and forms of narrative writing – as well, of course, as advanced work in historiography and the philosophy of history – are available'. This 'narrative turn' also resonates much more effectively with the training that the vast majority of business historians have experienced, reaffirming what Toms and Wilson (2017) noted as the principal characteristics of the discipline. Moreover, this work has not helped in encouraging a wider use of business history in terms of teaching and practical impact, prompting the need for a much wider consideration of issues beyond those of research methodology.

8.2 Building links with business

The debates surrounding methodological issues will no doubt continue, filling academic journals with more articles either denouncing the 'historic turn' in organization studies (Van Lent & Durepos, 2019a; pp. 1751–1752) or simply advocating 'plurality'. As we noted in Chapter 7, however, while this activity might well benefit reputations and personal contributions to exercises such as the UK Research Excellence Framework, it is still essential to seek a solution to what we perceive as a fundamental problem for the discipline of business history: while in research terms, we have seen a proliferation of activity by both historians and social scientists over the last forty years, in terms of the teaching and practical impact 'pillars' there has been a dearth of activity. One might even go further and argue that as many business historians are now employed in business schools, the pressures to research and publish in the social sciences could well engineer a reduction in business history research; even if the work is longitudinal in perspective, the orientation will increasingly be towards theoretical issues, regardless of the themes outlined earlier.

One of the most important questions that we asked in Chapter 1 was: 'Who should read business history?' An associated question would also be: 'How can business historians persuade students and practitioners of the value in reading their work?' At least since 1934, the BAC had been working effectively to preserve business archives and build links with those who relied primarily on this increasingly scarce resource. Over the last thirty years, several pioneers have also wrestled with the challenges associated with extending the discipline's readership, coming up with a range of solutions that have been at least partially successful. We noted in Section 2.1 that Glasgow University's Centre for Business History in Scotland was heavily supported by a private donation, while the base for the BHC, the Hagley Museum and Library is funded by the Du Pont Foundation. Similar developments were also to appear from the 1990s at Reading Business School (now the Henley Business School) and Nottingham University Business School, even if it is fair to note that both have struggled to make a significant contribution to either their institution's curricula or executive education. Unfortunately, however, while the LSE's Business History Unit showed great promise (see Section 2.3), and from 1989 Dr Terry Gourvish provided excellent leadership, generating several prestigious commissions from a government ministry (the Department of Transport), by 2014 it had been closed down by its home institution. Moreover, although several prominent practitioners joined the BHU, all of them were retired and had little influence with their firms, minimizing their contributions to initiating impact-related activities.

Section 2.1 also highlighted the work of Andrew Thomson and a few of his most senior colleagues at the Open University Business School (for example, Derek Pugh and Edward Brech) in establishing the Management History Research Group (MHRG). An essential prerequisite for their activities was the equal involvement of both practitioners and academics, resulting in the recruitment of several prominent businesspeople onto the management committee. Thomson also secured financial support from business leaders such as Sir John Bolton and Sir Adrian Cadbury, ensuring that a succession of seminars and workshops could be arranged. It was as a direct result of working together in the MHRG that Wilson and Thomson (2006) combined to write the first long-term history of British management, applying social science concepts to the empirical material as a means of appealing to business school academics when preparing their modules. Although the MHRG was later to evolve more into an organization dominated by academics, for a period between 1995 and 2008, there was a lively interchange between academics and practitioners on the subjects of management education and how best to utilize the burgeoning academic literature to bring a longer-term perspective to the way business is managed.

Another excellent British example of how the worlds of academia and practice can collide productively in the development of business and management is the Institute of Family Business (IFB). Founded in 2001, and directly affiliated with Family Business International, the IFB exists to support family businesses of every type and size as well as performing a lobbying function that ensures policymakers consider the interests of this dynamic community when devising and implementing business-related strategies. A key dimension of the IFB's organization is its Research Foundation, established as a registered charity in 2008 and now recognized as a major source of evidence on family firms and their impact across the economy and society. Crucially, the Research Foundation has collaborated extensively with several leading academics at universities in Dublin, Lancaster, Oxford and York, generating highly authoritative publications that are widely disseminated across the business and academic communities (IFB: Publications – Institute for Family Business (IFB)). This demonstrates the enormous potential in this kind of collaboration because rigorous academic research is applied directly to either improving the performance of family firms or highlighting their contributions to the British economy.

While it would be easy to idealize what the IFB and its associated Research Foundation have achieved over the last twenty years, at the very least they offer a glimpse of a solution to the challenges outlined earlier related to the way business history can improve its profile with regard to teaching and practical impact. In this context, we ought to refer to what is perhaps the most outstanding case of genuine interaction between business history and academia, the Gesellschaft für Unternehmensgeschichte e. V. (hereafter, GUG, *trans* Business History Society). Established in 1976, GUG has been characterized by a high level of co-operation between business and academia. Its original founders were representatives from prestigious corporations such as August Thyssen Hütte AG, Daimler Benz AG, Deutsche Bank

AG, Hoesch Werke AG, Mannesmann AG, Robert Bosch GmbH and Siemens AG, alongside Professor Wilhelm Treue as chairman of the executive board and Professor Hans Pohl as chairman of the academic advisory board. While it is fair to note that the academics were prompted to initiate this venture by the fear that their journal, *Tradition. Zeitschrift für Firmengeschichte (Tradition. Journal for Business History)* was about to be dropped by its publisher, the corporate founding members felt that highly respected academic research would correct what at the time was a negative image of entrepreneurs in the minds of many German citizens. This resulted in the development of public lectures as well as the revitalization of the journal as *Zeitschrift für Unternehmensgeschichte (Business History Journal,* or *ZUG*). Most importantly, however, in 1995 GUG opened up membership to individuals, while a dynamic new managing director was appointed in Dr. Andrea Schneider-Braunberger, who has provided creative leadership to the organization over the last twenty-five years.

To a large extent, GUG provides an excellent example of how business and business history can co-operate effectively, generating highly respected research that demonstrates how firms can deal with their past. Of major concern to the original founding corporate members was an honest and transparent analysis of the Nazi era when firms were linked intrinsically to a totalitarian regime that was responsible for a wide range of humanitarian horrors. A second major reason why GUG's services were sought was to celebrate significant anniversaries, while more recently the human resource implications of the COVID-19 pandemic has generated the need for authoritative analysis. At the core of this activity is the trust that GUG has built up with both business and the wider community because the research is conducted responsibly, objectively and thoroughly because Dr Schneider-Braunberger's team of twenty can recruit the best academics for the commissioned tasks. The organization also reflects German company law, in that an Executive Board runs GUG, while an Academic Advisory Council and a Board of Trustees provide appropriate oversight of the projects from both perspectives. Judging by the number of publications that GUG has produced over the last twenty-five years (mbH Publications (unternehmensgeschichte.de)) and the growing reputation of the journal *ZUG*, German business has certainly demonstrated its extensive trust in how they operate. More recently, GUG has also developed an archives service, advising many well-known firms on how best to preserve their records ARCHIVE (unternehmensgeschichte.de).

Whether or not the GUG model is transferable to other countries and replicate the kind of trust and projects that have been built up since the 1970s remains a source of intense debate. Certainly, Canadian business historians and significant corporations feel that this is possible because in 2015, the Canadian Business History Association – l'Association Canadienne pour l'Histoire des Affaires (CBHA/ACHA) – was formed. Taking advice from Dr Schneider-Braunberger, Professor Chris Kobrak recruited an impressive team of academics to lead the organization as well as persuading prominent corporations such as Canada Life, the Hudson's Bay Company and Bank of Montreal to provide business input. Operating out of the Rotman School of Management at the University of Toronto, CBHA/ACHA has already made a significant impact on the profile of business history in Canada. In 2021, The Wilson Foundation also pledged up to $2 million Canadian dollars to support CBHA/ACHA, clearly indicating how the GUG model has the potential to provide a major impetus to the way in which business historians can work productively with business, thereby enhancing the discipline's reputation. Indeed, Canada has proved to be a highly conducive environment for the Long Run Institute, a body founded in 2018 by John Turner, Laurence Mussio and Michael Aldous to connect decision-makers with 'the deep historical context that shapes complex challenges facing government and business' (About – The Long Run Institute). With the strapline 'Using the past to shape the future', the Institute has run a series of high-profile events that have involved business historians and leading businesspeople, thereby highlighting the extensive possibilities in this kind of interaction.

Having demonstrated how the GUG model is clearly having an impact on the profile of business history in two countries, it is nevertheless essential to assess whether these achievements are resolving the challenges associated with our two problematic 'pillars' of teaching and practical impact. To answer this question with regard to Germany, it is first of all necessary to understand the environment in which GUG has been operating. Specifically, German universities have not imitated the American and British predilection for establishing business schools, a feature that will significantly limit the ability of business historians to achieve much in terms of practical impact. Moreover, the study of economic history has undergone exactly the same process as in the United Kingdom, with student numbers declining rapidly and staff recruitment falling as a direct consequence. It would also be fair to note that in Canada the CBHA/ACHA has had limited success in converting business school deans to the cause of injecting business history into either curricula or executive development programmes, primarily because just like the United Kingdom and much of the United States, the discipline is largely regarded as peripheral to management education. While one might claim with some certainty that the GUG model offers a much richer future in terms of teaching and practical impact, the respective contexts fail to provide the kind of conducive environment that would result in all three of our 'pillars' being boosted. Even though the German and Canadian business communities have provided extensive support to these initiatives, and the research emanating from their teams has proved to be impressively analytical and thorough, other factors need to change if this model is to result in business history being a significant contributor to teaching and practical impact.

8.3 Conclusions

While some will no doubt refute this decidedly pessimistic view of the prospects for business history, pointing to the enormous literature that has been generated over the last forty years and the large number of business history conferences that now populate academics' diaries, it remains the case that outside a small number of elite institutions the discipline is marginalized, especially with regard to teaching and practical impact. Certainly, one can take heart from ventures such as GUG and CBHA/ACHA because they have successfully worked with major corporations to enhance the discipline's profile. One might even go so far as to argue that had the German university system been more like that of the United States or the United Kingdom, GUG would have been capable of achieving success across all three of our 'pillars'. This claim highlights a feature that perhaps ought to be replicated across all business history associations and research clusters because by aligning with business interests, as well as policymakers, business historians would be much better placed to claim the legitimacy to which most aspire in the eyes of academia generally. Of course, there are dangers associated with this solution, in that many academics would resist direct involvement in research by business or government as inherently dangerous, potentially undermining objective analysis and limiting access to crucial records. As GUG has demonstrated, however, as long as the nature of the business-academia relationship is transparent and agreed upon at the outset, then these dangers can be avoided, resulting in high-quality research that can be fed into curricula and impact activities. Academia has little to fear if it enters into arrangements that provide for an effective two-way interchange of ideas, analysis and recommendations, a claim substantiated by not only GUG's achievements but also the work of the IFB and early years of the MHRG.

Building on this proposal, we would also encourage the discipline to engage more extensively with some fresh agendas. Specifically, we anticipate that the following would merit much greater attention:

- *Emerging Markets*: we agree with Friedman and Jones (2017; p. 455), who strongly encourage business historians to engage in research projects that encompass economies outside the United States, Western Europe and Japan; 'the future of business history rests in part on recognizing the centrality of this alternative business history, rather than treating the business history of Africa, Asia, and Latin America as tangential to the central themes of the discipline'. Scranton (2019, 2020) has already made this move, putting into practice what he and Fridenson (2013) noted in *Reimagining Business History*.
- *Sustainability*: while Jones and Lubinski (2014; p. 18) made a strenuous appeal for business historians to analyse 'why some firms become "greener" than others', apart from the work of Bergquist (2017) and a very small group of business historians, relatively little effort has been made to develop this theme and assess the wide sustainability agenda and corporate responses. The forthcoming book by Jones (2022) will no doubt stimulate much wider interest in the role business has played in accommodating the environmental agenda into corporate strategy and performance, focusing especially on the term 'deep responsibility'.
- *Corporate Ethics and Corporate Governance:* as we noted towards the end of Section 2.2, while there has been extensive work done in these fields, given the extent of corporate misbehaviour and violations of corporate codes it is vital that business historians participate in these debates. For example, the British Academy's *Future of the Corporation* project (2021) would benefit from greater historical insights into context and behaviour.
- *Gender and Race:* again, while the literature on women and racial issues in business has expanded over the course of the last thirty years, these remain significant areas for investigation because of the way they open up our understanding of how business and society interact. One might also add that masculinity is another neglected area of study; even though sociologists have written extensively about 'hegemonic masculinity' (Connell & Wood, 2005), the business history literature has failed to assess how this influenced the achievement and execution of power.

These are but four of the research fields to which the discipline could contribute extensively over the next decade. Above all, though, returning to the main theme of the chapter, we feel that it is insufficient merely to generate academic research on these and any other issues; what the discipline needs to do is align itself more closely with the worlds of practice, whether it be business or policymaking, bringing their representatives into research projects, conferences, workshops and seminars in order to demonstrate the intrinsic value of business history in opening up fresh vistas. To reiterate what was noted in Chapter 1, *we regard business history as a window on key aspects of society and human activity, providing a rich, nuanced, empirically based understanding of how business interacts with and influences the world around it.* It is this richness that is at times missing from the theory-oriented social sciences and certainly from the leading MOS journals that only publish articles which contribute to theory, making them inaccessible to the worlds of practice. We venture to argue that in aligning itself to the needs of practitioners and bringing them more extensively into its activities, business history can contribute effectively to teaching and impact-related work, thereby enhancing both management education and our view of the world as it evolves.

References

Acemoglu, D., Johnson, S., & Robinson, J.A. (2001). The colonial origins of comparative development: An empirical investigation. *American Economic Review, 91*(5), 1369–1401.

Acheson, Graeme G., Campbell, G., & Turner, John D. (2015). Active controllers or wealthy rentiers? Large shareholders in Victorian public companies. *Business History Review, 89*(4), 661–691.

Acheson, Graeme G., Coyle, C., & Turner, John D. (2016). Happy hour followed by hangover: Financing the UK brewery industry, 1880–1913. *Business History, 58*(5), 725–751.

Acheson, Graeme G., Campbell, G., & Turner, John D. (2017). Who financed the expansion of the equity market? Shareholder clienteles in Victorian Britain. *Business History, 59*(4), 607–637.

Acheson, Graeme G., Campbell, G., & Turner, John D. (2019). Private contracting, law and finance. *The Review of Financial Studies, 32*(11), 4156–4195.

Adkins, E., & Benedict, K. (2011). Archival advocacy: Institutional archives in corporations. In L. Hackman (Ed.), *Many Happy Returns: Advocacy and the Development of Archives* (pp. 45–66). Chicago, IL: Society of American Archivists.

Adler, N.J., & Harzing, A.W. (2009). When knowledge wins: Transcending the sense and nonsense in academic ranking. *Academy of Management Learning & Education, 8*, 72–95.

Aguinis, H., Gottfredson, R.K., Culpepper, S.A., Dalton, D.R., & de Bruin, G.P. (2013). Doing good and doing well: On the multiple contributions of journal editors. *Academy of Management Learning & Education, 12*, 564–578.

Aldous, M., & Conroy, K.M. (2021). Navigating institutional change: An historical perspective of firm responses to pro-market reversals. *Journal of International Management, 27*(2), 100849.

Alford, B.W.E. (1973). *W. D. & H. O. Wills and the Development of the UK Tobacco Industry: 1786–1965*. London: Methuen.

Alford, B.W.E. (1976). Strategy and structure in the UK tobacco industry. In L. Hannah (Ed.), *Management Strategy and Business Development* (pp. 73–84). London: Methuen.

Alford, B.W.E. (1977). Entrepreneurship, business performance and industrial development. *Business History*, *19*(2), 116–133.

Álvaro-Moya, A., & Donzé, P. (2016). Business history and management studies. *Journal of Evolutionary Studies in Business*, *1*(1), 122–151.

Alvesson, M., Gabriel, Y., & Paulsen, R. (2021). *Return to Meaning: A Social Science with Something to Say*. Oxford: Oxford University Press.

Amatori, F., & Colli, A. (2007). Strategies and structures of European enterprise. *Revue Économique*, *58*(1), 39–57.

Amatori, F., & Colli, A. (2011). *Business History. Complexities and Comparisons*, Abingdon: Routledge.

Anderson, H. (1982). Business archives: A corporate asset. *The American Archivist*, *45*(3), 264–266.

Andrews, T., & Burke, F. What does it mean to think historically?, *Perspectives in History* (2007). http://www.historians.org/publications-and directories/perspectives-on-history/january-2007/what-does-it-mean-to-thinkhistorically

Anson, M. (2010). 'History in firms' documents': 75 years of the Business Archives Council. *Business Archives*, *100*, 1–11.

Anteby, M., & Molnár, V. (2012). Collective memory meets organizational identity: Remembering to forget in a firm's rhetorical history. *Academy of Management Journal*, *55*(3), 515–540.

Aohi, N. (2012). Japanese traditional industries and archives: The case of Toraya confectionery. In Shibusawa Eiichi Memorial Foundation (Ed.), *Leveraging Corporate Assets: New Global Directions for Business Archives* (pp. 11–26). Tokyo: Shibusawa Eiichi Memorial Foundation.

Argyres, Nicholas S., De Massis, A., Foss, Nicolai J., Frattini, F., Jones, G., & Silverman, Brian S. (2020). History-informed strategy research: The promise of history and historical research methods in advancing strategy scholarship. *Strategic Management Journal*, *41*(3), 343–368.

Ashley, W. (1914). *The Economic Organisation of England: An Outline History*. London: Longmans, Green & Co.

Bailey, J., & Ford, C. (1996). Management as science versus management as practice in postgraduate business education. *Business Strategy Review*, *7*(4), 7–12.

Barker, T.C. (1960). *Pilkington Brothers and the Glass Industry*. London: Allen & Unwin.

Barker, T.C. (1976), 'A family firm becomes a public company: Changes at Pilkington Brothers Ltd in the interwar years'. In L. Hannah (Ed.), *Management Strategy and Business Development*. London: Methuen, pp. 85–94.

Bartunek, J., & Rynes, S. (2010). The construction and contributions of 'implications for practice': What's in them and what might they offer? *Academy of Management Learning and Education*, *9*(1), 100–117.

Bartunek, J., Rynes, S., & Ireland, R.D. (2006). What makes management research interesting and why does it matter? *Academy of Management Journal*, *49*, 9–15.

Basque, J., & Langley, A. (2018). Invoking Alphonse: The founder figure as a historical resource for organizational identity work. *Organization Studies, 39*(12), 1685–1708.

Batiz-Lazo, B. (2019). What is new in "a new history of management"? *Journal of Management History, 25*(1), 114–124.

Beckmann, R., Gillespie, N., & Priem, R. (2015). Repairing trust in Organizations and Institutions: Toward a conceptual framework. *Organization Studies, 36*(9), 1123–1142.

Bergquist, A. (2017). 'Business and sustainability: New business history perspectives. Harvard Business School Working Paper, 18–034.

Berle, A., & Means, G. (1932). *Private Property and the Modern Corporation.* New York: Macmillan.

Bieri, A. (2012). The DNA of corporations: A key enabler for success. In Shibusawa Eiichi Memorial Foundation (Ed.), *Leveraging Corporate Assets: New Global Directions for Business Archives* (pp. 39–52). Tokyo: Shibusawa Eiichi Memorial Foundation.

Blagoev, B., Felten, S., & Kahn, R. (2018). The career of a catalogue: Organizational memory, materiality and the dual nature of the past at the British Museum (1970–Today). *Organization Studies, 39*(12), 1757–1783.

Booth, C., Clark, P., Delahaye, A., Procter, S., & Rowlinson, M. (2007). Accounting for the dark side of corporate history: Organizational culture perspectives and the Bertelsmann case. *Critical Perspectives on Accounting, 18*(6), 625–644.

Bowden, B. (2018). *Work, Wealth, and Postmodernism: The Intellectual Conflict at the Heart of Business Endeavour.* Cham: Palgrave Macmillan.

Bowden, B. (2020). The historic (wrong) turn in management and organizational studies. *Journal of Management History, 27*(1), 8–27.

Bridgman, T., Cummings, S., & McLaughlin, C. (2016). Restating the case: How revisiting the development of the case method can help us think differently about the future of the business school. *Academy of Management Learning & Education, 15*(4), 724–741.

British Academy (2021). *Future of the Corporation.* https://www.thebritishacademy.ac.uk/programmes/future-of-the-corporation/

Bromiley, P., & Fleming, L. (2002). The resource-based view of strategy: A behaviourist critique. In M. Augier & J.G. March (Eds.), *The Economics of Choice, Change and Organization: Essays in Memory of Richard M. Cyert* (p. 319). Herndon, VA: Edward Elgar Publishing.

Brunninge, O. (2009). Using history in organizations: How managers make purposeful reference to history in strategy processes. *Journal of Organizational Change Management, 22*(1), 8–26.

Bucheli, M., Salvaj, E., & Kim, M. (2019). Better together: How multinationals come together with business groups in times of economic and political transitions. *Global Strategy Journal, 9*(2), 176–207.

Bucheli, M., & Wadhwani, D. (Eds.) (2014). , *Organizations in Time. History, Theory, Methods.* Oxford: Oxford University Press.

Buchnea, E., Wong, N., & Wilson, J. (2020). The "historic turn" in management teaching? The integration of history into business schools. *Academy of Management Proceedings, 2020*(1), 20474.

Buckley, P.J. (2016). Historical research approaches to the analysis of internationalisation. *Management International Review, 56*(6), 879–900.

Buckley, P.J. (2020). The role of history in international business: Evidence, research practices, methods and theory. *British Journal of Management, 32*(3), 797–811.

Buckley, P.J., & Casson, M. (2021). Thirty years of International Business Review and international business research. *International Business Review, 30*(2), 1–24.

Buckley, P.J., & Pérez, P.F. (2016). The role of history in international business in southern Europe. *Journal of Evolutionary Studies in Business, 1*(2), 1–13.

Burke, L.A., & Rau, B. (2010). The research–teaching gap in management. *Academy of Management Learning & Education, 9*(1), 132–143.

Cailluet, L., Gorge, H., & Özçağlar-Toulouse, N. (2018). 'Do not expect me to stay quiet': Challenges in managing a historical strategic resource. *Organization Studies, 39*(12), 1811–1835.

Carney, M. (2020). https://www.thinkunthink.org/latest-unthinking/2020-07-22-mark-carney-past-crises-teach-us-to-put-people-and-planet-first

Casson, M. (1994). Institutional diversity in overseas enterprise: Explaining the free-standing company. *Business History, 46*, 407–438.

Castellani, P., & Rossato, C. (2014). On the communication value of the company museum and archives. *International Journal of Information and Communication Technology Education, 18*(3), 240–253.

Chandler, A.D., Jr. (1956). Management decentralization: An historical analysis. *Business History Review, 30*(2), 111–174.

Chandler, A.D., Jr. (1962). *Strategy and Structure: Chapters in the History of the Industrial Enterprise.* Boston, MA: MIT Press.

Chandler, A.D. & Daems, H. (Eds.). (1974). *The Rise of Managerial Capitalism.* Louvain: Louvain University Press.

Chandler, A.D. (1976). 'The development of modern management structure in the US and UK. In L. Hannah (Ed.), *Management Strategy and Business Development.* London: Methuen, pp. 23–51.

Chandler A.D. (1977). *The visible hand.* Cambridge MA: Harvard University Press.

Chandler, A.D. (1978). Presidential Address, 1978: Business History — A Personal Experience. *Business and Economic History: Papers Presented at the… Annual Meeting of the Business History Conference. Business History Conference, 7*, 1–8.

Chandler, A.D. (1990). *Scale and Scope: The Dynamics of Industrial Capitalism.* Cambridge, MA: Harvard University Press.

Channon, D.F. (1973), *The Strategy and Structure of British Enterprise.* London: Macmillan.

Cheffins, B.R. (2008), *Corporate Ownership and Control. British Business Transformed.* Oxford: Oxford University Press.

Chia, R., & Holt, R. (2009). *Strategy without Design: The Silent Efficacy of Indirect Action*. Cambridge: Cambridge University Press.

Chihadeh, C. (2020). Towards critical historical studies: An emancipatory ontology. In M. Maclean, S.R. Clegg, R. Suddaby, & C. Harvey (Eds.), *Historical Organization Studies: Theory and Applications* (pp. 78–89). London: Routledge.

Clark, P., & Rowlinson, M. (2004). The treatment of history in organization studies: Towards an 'historic turn'? *Business History*, *46*(3), 331–352.

Coleman, D. (1969). *Courtaulds: An Economic and Social History*. Oxford: Clarendon Press.

Coleman, D. (1987). The uses and abuses of business history. *Business History*, *29*(2), 141–156.

Coller, K., Mills, J., & Mills, A. (2016). The British Airways heritage collection: An ethnographic 'history'. *Business History*, *58*(4), 547–570.

Connell, R.W., & Wood, J. (2005). Globalization and business masculinities. *Men and Masculinities*, *7*(4), 347–364.

Cook, F.W. (1926). Charter of The Business Historical Society, Incorporated. *Bulletin of the Business Historical Society*, *1*(1), 11–16.

Coraiola, D.M., & Derry, R. (2020). Remembering to forget: The historic Irresponsibility of U.S. Big Tobacco. *Journal of Business Ethics: JBE*, *166*(2), 233–252.

Coraiola, D., Foster, W.M., & Suddaby, R. (2015). Varieties of history in organization studies. In P. Genoe, M. McLaren, A. Mills, & T.G. Weatherbee (Eds.), *The Routledge Companion to Management & Organizational History* (pp. 206–221). Abingdon: Routledge.

Corrigan, L. T. (2016). Accounting practice and the historic turn: performing budget histories. *Management & Organizational History*, *11*(2), 77–98.

Cummings, S., & Bridgman, T. (2011). The relevant past: Why the history of management should be critical for our future. *Academy of Management Learning & Education*, *10*(1), 77–93.

Cummings, S., & Bridgman, T. (2016). The limits and possibilities of history: How a wider, deeper, and more engaged understanding of business history can foster innovative thinking. *Academy of Management Learning & Education*, *15*, 250–267.

Cummings, S., Bridgman, T., Hassard, J., & Rowlinson, M. (2017). *A New History of Management*. Cambridge: Cambridge University Press.

da Silva Lopes, T., Casson, M., & Jones, G. (2019). Organizational innovation in the multinational enterprise: Internalization theory and business history. *Journal of International Business Studies*, *50*(8), 1338–1358.

David, P.A. (1985). Clio and the economics of QWERTY. *The American Economic Review*, *75*(2), 332–337.

de Jong, A., & Higgins, D. (Eds.). (2015). New business history? *Business History* special issue *57*(1), 1–4.

de Jong, A., Higgins, D., & van Driel, H. (2015). Towards a new business history? *Business History*, *57*(1), 5–29.

Decker, S. (2013). The silence of the archives: Business history, post-colonialism and archival ethnography. *Management & Organizational History*, *8*(2), 155–173.

Decker, S. (2016). Paradigms lost: Integrating history and organization studies. *Management & Organizational History*, *11*(4), 364–379.

Decker, S. (2016a). Mothership reconnection: Microhistory and institutional work compared. In P. Genoe, M. McLaren, A. Mills, & T.G. Weatherbee (Eds.), *The Routledge Companion to Management and Organizational History* (pp. 222–237). Abingdon: Routledge.

Decker, S. (2018). Africanization in British Multinationals in Ghana and Nigeria, 1945–1970. *Business History Review*, *92*(4), 691–718.

Decker, S., Hassard, J., & Rowlinson, M. (2020). Rethinking history and memory in organization studies: The case for historiographical reflexivity. *Human Relations*. doi:10.1177/0018726720927443

Decker, S., Kipping, M., & Wadhwani, D. (2015). New business histories! Plurality in business history research methods. *Business History*, *57*(1), 30–40.

Demil, Benoît. (2020). Reintroducing public actors in entrepreneurial dynamics: A co-evolutionary approach to categorization. *Strategic Entrepreneurship Journal*, *14*(1), 43–65.

Devine, P.J., Lee, N., Jones, R.M., & Tyson, W.J. (4th ed. 1985). *An Introduction to Industrial Economics*. London: Unwin Hyman.

Dobbin, F. (1994). *Forging Industrial Policy: The United States, Britain, and France in the railway age*. Cambridge: Cambridge University Press.

Dominguez, N., & Mayrhofer, U. (2017). Internationalization stages of traditional SMEs: Increasing, decreasing and re-increasing commitment to foreign markets. *International Business Review*, *26*(6), 1051–1063.

Downie, J. (1958). *The Competitive Process*. London: Duckworth.

Durepos, G., Mills, A. J., & Helms Mills, J. (2008). Tales in the manufacture of knowledge: Writing a business history of Pan American airlines, *Management & Organizational History*, *3*(1), 63–80.

Durepos, G., & Mills, A.J. (2012). Actor-network theory, ANTi-history and critical organizational historiography. *Organization*, *19*(6), 703–721.

Durepos, G., & Mills, A.J. (2018). Anti-history: An alternative approach to history. In C. Cassell, A.L. Cunliffe, & G. Grandy (Eds.), *The SAGE Handbook of Qualitative Business and Management Research Methods: Methods and Challenges* (pp. 431–448). London: SAGE Publications Ltd.

Durepos, G., & Vince, R. (2020). Towards a theory of historical reflexivity. In M. Maclean, S.R. Clegg, R. Suddaby, & C. Harvey (Eds.), *Historical Organization Studies: Theory and Applications* (pp. 39–56). London: Routledge.

Durepos, G., Maclean, M., Alcadipani, R., & Cummings, S. (2020). Historical reflections at the intersection of past and future: Celebrating 50 years of Management Learning. *Management Learning*, *51*(1), 3–16.

Dyas, G.P., & Tanheiser, H.T. (1974), *The Emerging European Enterprise. Strategy and Structure in French and German Industry*. London: Macmillan.

Edelman. (2021). Edelman Trust Barometer. New York: Edelman Associates. https://www.edelman.com/sites/g/files/aatuss191/files/2021-01/2021-edelman-trust-barometer.pdf

Edgerton, D. (1997). The decline of declinism. *Business History Review, 71*(2), 201–206.

Fellman, S., & Popp, A. (2013). Lost in the archive: The business historian in distress. In B. Czarniawska & O. Löfgren (Eds.), *Coping with Excess* (pp. 216–243). Cheltenham: Edward Elgar Publishing.

Financial Reporting Council (FRC) (2019). The Annual Review of Corporate Governance and Reporting. https://www.frc.org.uk/getattachment/f70e56b9-7daf-4248-a1ae-a46bad67c85e/Annual-Review-of-CG-R-241018.pdf

Fligstein, N. (2008). *The Transformation of Corporate Control.* Boston, MA: Harvard University Press.

Fligstein, N. (2008a). Chandler and the Sociology of Organizations. *Business History Review, 82*(2), 241–250.

Force, D.C. (2014). The admissibility of business records as legal evidence: A review of the business records exception to the Hearsay Rule in Canada. *Archivaria, 78*(0), 25–51.

Force, M. (2009). Company history: Corporate archives' Public Outreach on Fortune 100 Company Websites. *Provenance, Journal of the Society of Georgia Archivists, 27*(1), 24–50.

Foreman-Peck, J. & Hannah, L. (2013). Some consequences of the early twentieth century British divorce of ownership from control. *Business History, 55*(4), 543–564.

Foreman-Peck, J., Raff, D., & Scott, P. (2019). Introduction: Leslie Hannah and the business history in his time. *Business History* special issue 'Leslie Hannah Festschrift', *61*(7), 1091–1107.

Foroughi, H., Coraiola, D.M., Rintamäki, J., Mena, S., & Foster, W.M. (2020). Organizational memory studies. *Organization Studies, 41*(12), 1725–1748.

Foster, W.M., Suddaby, R., Minkus, A., & Wiebe, E. (2011). History as social memory assets: The example of Tim Hortons. *Management & Organizational History, 6*(1), 101–120.

Freeland, R.F. (1993). *The Struggle for Control of the Modern Corporation: Organizational Change at General Motors, 1924–1970.* Cambridge: Cambridge University Press.

Friedman, W.A., & Jones, G. (2012). *Guide to Business History Courses Worldwide.* Boston, MA: Harvard Business School.

Friedman, W.A., & Jones, G. (2017). Time for debate. *Business History Review, 85*(Spring 2017), 1–8.

Fruin, M. (1992). *The Japanese Enterprise System.* Oxford: Oxford University Press.

Galambos, L. (2010). The role of professionals in the Chandler Paradigm. *Industrial and Corporate Change, 19*(2), 377–398.

Gardner, D. (1982). Commentary I I. *American Archivist, 45*(3), 294–295.

Gioia, D.A., Corley, K.G., & Fabbri, T. (2002). Revising the past (while thinking in the future perfect tense). *Journal of Organizational Change Management, 15*(6), 622–634.

Godfrey, Paul C., Hassard, J., O'Connor, Ellen S., Rowlinson, M., & Ruef, M. (2016). What is organizational history? Toward a creative synthesis of history and organization studies. *The Academy of Management Review, 41*(4), 590–608.

Godley, A.C., & Hamilton, S. (2020). Different expectations: A comparative history of structure, experience, and strategic alliances in the U.S. and U.K. poultry sectors, 1920–1990. *Strategic Entrepreneurship Journal, 14*(1), 89–104.

Gras, N.S.B., & Larson, H.M. (1939). *Casebook in American business history.* Bloomington: Appleton Century Crofts Inc.

Gray, V. (2002). Developing the corporate memory: The potential of business archives. *Business Information Review, 19*(1), 32–37.

Green, A.R., & Lee, E. (2020). From transaction to collaboration: Redefining the academic-archivist relationship in business collections. *Archives and Records, 41*(1), 32–51.

Hagund Tousey, B. (2012). Proud heritage: The use of heritage stories in the past. In Shibusawa Eiichi Memorial Foundation (Ed.), *Leveraging Corporate Assets: New Global Directions for Business Archives* (pp. 79–86). Tokyo: Shibusawa Eiichi Memorial Foundation.

Haley, U.C.V. (2018). Beyond impact factors: An academy of management report on measuring scholarly impact, Impact of Social Sciences Blog. London School of Economics. https://blogs.lse.ac.uk/impactofsocialsciences/2018/03/02/beyond-impact-factors-an-academy-of-management-report-on-measuring-scholarly-impact/

Haley, U.C.V., Cooper, C., Hoffman, A., Pitsis, T., Greenberg, D., & Hibbert, P. (2021). Learning and education strategies for scholarly impact: Influencing regulation, policy and society through research, Academy of Management Learning & Education, Call for papers, Microsoft Word - AMLE Special Issue Call.docx (aom.org).

Hall, R.L., & Hitch, C.J. (1939). Price theory and business behaviour. *Oxford Economic Papers, 2*(1), 12–45.

Hambrick, D.C. (2007). The field of management's devotion to theory: Too much of a good thing?. *Academy of Management Journal, 50*, 1346–1352.

Hannah, L. (1976, 1983). *The Rise of the Corporate Economy.* London: Methuen & Co Ltd.

Hannah, L. (1976a). Business development and economic structure in the US and UK. In L. Hannah (Ed.), *Management Strategy and Business Development.* London: Methuen.

Hannah, L. (1983). New issues in British business history. *Business History Review, 57*(2), 165–174.

Hannah, L. (1999). Marshall's "Trees" and the Global "Forest": Were "Giant Redwoods" Different? In Naomi R. Lamoreaux, Daniel M.G. Raff & Peter Temin (Eds.), *Learning by Doing in Markets, Firms, and Countries* (pp. 253–294). Chicago, IL: University of Chicago Press.

Hannah, L. (2009). Strategic games, scale, an efficiency, or Chandler goes to Hollywood 1. In R. Coopey & P. Lyth (Eds.), *Business in Britain in the Twentieth Century: Decline and Renaissance?* (p. 21). Oxford: Oxford University Press. https://oxford.universitypressscholarship.com/view/10.1093/acprof:oso/9780199226009.001.0001/acprof-9780199226009-chapter-2?print=pdf.

Hannah, L., & Kay, J.A. (1977) *Concentration in Modern Industry: Theory, Measurement and the UK Experience*. London: The Macmillan Press Ltd.

Hansen, P.H. (2007). Organizational culture and organizational change: The transformation of savings banks in Denmark, 1965–1990. *Enterprise & Society, 8*(4), 920–953.

Harvey, C., Maclean, M., Gordon, J., & Shaw, E. (2011). Andrew Carnegie and the foundations of contemporary entrepreneurial philanthropy. *Business History, 53*(3), 425–450.

Hatch, M.J., & Schultz, M. (2017). Toward a theory of using history authentically: Historicizing in the Carlsberg Group. *Administrative Science Quarterly, 62*(4), 1–41.

Hielscher, S., & Husted, B.W. (2020). Proto-CSR before the industrial revolution: Institutional experimentation by medieval miners' Guilds. *Journal of Business Ethics: JBE, 166*(2), 253–269.

Higgins, D., Toms, S., & Filatotchev, I. (2015). Ownership, financial strategy and performance: The Lancashire cotton textile industry, 1918–1938. *Business History, 57* (1), 96–121.

Hills, S., Voronov, M., & Hinings, C.R. (bob). (2013). Putting new wine in old bottles: Utilizing rhetorical history to overcome stigma associated with a previously dominant logic. In M. Lounsbury, & E. Boxenbaum (Eds.), *Research in the Sociology of Organizations: Vol. 39 Part B. Institutional Logics in Action, Part B* (pp. 99–137). Bingley: Emerald Group Publishing.

Hoffman, A. (2016). Academia's emerging crisis of relevance and the consequent role of the engaged scholar. *Journal of Change Management, 16*(2), 77–96.

Hollow, M. (2020). Historicizing entrepreneurial networks. *Strategic Entrepreneurship Journal, 14*(1), 66–88.

Holt, D.B. (2006). Jack Daniel's America: Iconic brands as ideological parasites and proselytizers. *Journal of Consumer Culture, 6*(3), 355–377.

Hoskin, K., & Macve, R. (1994). Reappraising the genesis of managerialism: A re-examination of the role of accounting at the Springfield Armory, 1815–1845. *Accounting, Auditing & Accountability Journal, 7*(2), 4–29.

Hudson, L., & Mansfield, I. (2020). Universities at the crossroads, policy exchange. https://policyexchange.org.uk/publication/universities-at-the-crossroads/

Hughes, T., Bence, D., Grisoni. L., O'Regan & Wornham, D. (2011). Scholarship that Matters: Academic-Practitioner Engagement in Business and Management. *Academy of Management Learning & Education, 10*(1), 40–57.

Iglesias, O., Ind, N., & Schultz, M. (2020). History matters: The role of history in corporate brand strategy. *Business Horizons, 63*(1), 51–60.

Ingram, P., Rao, H., & Silverman, B.S. (2012). History in strategy research: What, why and how?' In S.J. Kahl, B.S. Silverman, & M.A. Cusumano

(Eds.), *History and Strategy* (pp. 241–273). Bingley: Emerald Group Publishing Limited.

Jensen, M.C. (1993). The modern industrial revolution, exit, and the failure of internal control systems. *Journal of Finance, 48*(3), 831–880.

Jeremy, D.J. (1998). *A Business History of Britain, 1900–1990s*. Oxford: Oxford University Press.

Jeremy, D.J. (2002). Business history and strategy. In A. Pettigrew, H. Thomas & R. Whittington (Eds.), *Handbook of Strategy and Management* (pp. 436–460). London: Sage Publications.

Jeremy, D.J., & Tweedale, G. (2005). *Business history*. London: Sage Library in Business and Management.

Johanson, J., & Vahlne, J.E. (1977). The internationalization process of the firm—A model of knowledge development and increasing foreign market commitments. *Journal of International Business Studies, 8*(1), 23–32.

Jones, G. (1996). *The Evolution of International Business: An Introduction*. London: Routledge.

Jones, G. (2017). Business history, the great divergence and the great convergence. Harvard Business School Working Paper, 18-004.

Jones, G. (2021). Renewing the relevance of IB: Can some history help?. In A. Verbeke, R. van Tulder, E.L. Rose, & Y. Wei (Eds.), *The Multiple Dimensions of Institutional Complexity in International Business Research*. Emerald Publishing Limited.

Jones, G. (2022). *The Search for the Deep Responsibility of Business*. Boston, MA: Harvard University Press.

Jones, G., & Friedman, W. (2017). Debating methodology in business history. *Business History Review, 91*(Autumn 2017), 443–455.

Jones, G., & Khanna, T. (2006). Bringing history (back) into international business. *Journal of International Business Studies, 37*(4), 453–468.

Jones, G., & Sluyterman, K.E. (2003). British and Dutch business history. In F. Amatori & G. Jones (Eds.), *Business History around the World* (pp. 111–145). Cambridge: Cambridge University Press.

Jones, G., & Zeitlin, J. (2007). Introduction. In G. Jones & J. Zeitlin (Eds.), *The Oxford Handbook of Business History* (pp. 1–8). Oxford University Press.

Jones, G., & Lubinski, C. (2014). Making 'Green Giants': Environment sustainability in the German chemical industry, 1950s–1980s. *Business History, 56*(4), 1–14.

Kahl, S.J., Silverman, B.S., & Cusumano, M.A. (2012). The integration of history and strategy research. In S.J. Kahl, B.S. Silverman, & M.A. Cusumano (Eds.), *In History and Strategy* (pp. ix–xxi). Bingley: Emerald Group Publishing Limited.

Katriel, T. (1994). Sites of memory: Discourses of the past in Israeli pioneering settlement museums. *Quarterly Journal of Speech, 80*(1), 1–20.

Kay, J. (2012). *Lessons from the house that Lewis built*. https://www.johnkay.com/2012/04/04/lessons-from-the-house-that-lewis-built/

Kedia, B.L., & Bilgili, T.V. (2015). When history matters: The effect of historical ties on the relationship between institutional distance and shares acquired. *International Business Review, 24*(6), 921–934.

Kemal Ataman, B. (2009). Archives mean money: How to make the most of archives for public relations public relations purposes -The Yapi Kredi Bank Example. *Source: The American Archivist, 72*(1), 197–213.

Kennedy, W.P., & Payne, P. (1976), 'Directions for future research'. In L. Hannah (Ed.), *Management Strategy and Business Development*. London: Methuen, pp. 237–258.

Kieser, A. (1994). Why organization theory needs historical analyses—And how this should be performed. *Organization Science, 5*(4), 608–620.

Kieser, A., & Leiner, L. (2009). Why the rigor-relevance gap in management research in unbridgeable. *Journal of Management Studies, 13*, 97–108.

Kipping, M., & Üsdiken, B. (2014). History in organization and management theory: More than meets the eye. *Annals, 8*(1), 535–588.

Kipping, M., Kurosawa, T., & Wadhwani, R.D. (2016). A revisionist historiography of business history: A richer past for a richer future. In J. Wilson, S. Toms, A. de Jong, & E. Buchnea (Eds.), *The Routledge Companion to Business History* (pp. 19–35). Abingdon: Routledge.

Kluppel, L., Pierce, L., & Snyder, J. (2018). The deep historical roots of organization and strategy: Traumatic shocks, culture and institutions. *Organization Science, 29*(4), 702–721.

Kobrak, C., Oesterle, M.J., & Röber, B. (2018). Escape FDI and the varieties of capitalism: Why history matters in international business. *Management International Review, 58*(3), 449–464.

Kondrat, M.E. (1995). Concept, act and interest in professional practice: Implications of an empowerment perspective. *Social Service Review, 69*, 405–428.

Kraimer, M.L., Greco, L., Seibert, S.E., & Sargent, L.D. (2019). An investigation of academic career success: The new tempo of academic life. *Academy of Management Learning & Education, 18*(2), 128–152.

Lamond, D. (2005). On the value of management history. *Management Decision, 43*(10), 1273–1281.

Lamoreaux, N.R., Raff, D.M.G., & Temin, P. (2003). Beyond markets and hierarchies: Toward a new synthesis of American business history. *American Historical Review, 108*, April, 404–433.

Lamoreaux, Naomi R., Raff, Daniel M.G., & Temin, P. (2004). Against whig history. *Enterprise & Society 5*(3), 376–387.

Lamoreaux, N., Raff, D., & Temin, P. (2007). Business history and economic theory. In G. Jones & J. Zeitlin (Eds.), *The Oxford Handbook of Business History*. Oxford: Oxford University Press.

Langlois, R.N. (2004). Chandler in a larger frame: Markets, transaction costs, and organizational form in history. *Enterprise & Society, 5*(3), 355–375.

Langlois, R.N. & Robertson, P.L. (1995). *Firms, Markets, and Economic Change: A Dynamic Theory of Business Institutions*. London: Routledge.

Lasewicz, P.C. (2015). Forget the past? Or history matters? Selected academic perspectives on the strategic value of organizational pasts. *The American Archivist, 78*(1), 59–83.

Latour, B. (1987). Science *In Action: How To Follow Scientists And Engineers Through Society.* Cambridge, MA: Harvard University Press.

Lazonick, W. (2002). Organizational learning and international competition: The skill-base hypothesis. In W. Lazonick & M. O'Sullivan (Eds.), *Corporate Governance and Sustainable Prosperity* (pp. 37–77). London: Palgrave Macmillan:.

Lazonick, W. (2010). The Chandlerian corporation and the theory of innovative enterprise. *Industrial and Corporate Change, 19*(2), 317–349.

Lazonick, W. (2015). Stock buybacks: From retain-and-reinvest to downsize-and-distribute, Centre for Effective Public Management at Brookings, April, pp. 1–22.

Leblebici, H. (2014). History and organization theory: Potential for a transdisciplinary convergence. In M. Bucheli & R. D. Wadhwani (Eds.), *Organizations in Time: History, Theory and Methods* (pp. 56–98). Oxford: Oxford University Press.

Lee, C. (1990). Corporate behaviour in theory and history: I The evolution of theory. *Business History, 32*(1), 17–27.

Lee, C. (1990a). Corporate behaviour in theory and history: II The historian's perspective. *Business History, 32*(2), 177–190.

Lippmann, S., & Aldrich, H.E. (2014). History and evolutionary theory. In M. Bucheli, & R.D. Wadhwani (Eds.), *Organizations in Time: History, Theory Methods* (pp. 124–146). Oxford: Oxford University Press.

Lippmann, S., & Aldrich, H.E. (2016). A rolling stone gathers momentum: Generational units, collective memory, and entrepreneurship. *Academy of Management Review.* https://journals.aom.org/doi/abs/10.5465/amr.2014.0139

Lubinski, C. (2018). From 'history as told' to 'history as experienced': Contextualizing the uses of the past. *Organization Studies, 39*(12), 1785–1809.

Lubinski, C., & Wadhwani, R.D. (2020). Geopolitical jockeying: Economic nationalism and multinational strategy in historical perspective. *Strategic Management Journal, 41*(3), 400–422.

Luyckx, J., & Janssens, M. (2016). Discursive legitimation of a contested actor over time: The multinational corporation as a historical case (1964–2012). *Organization Studies, 37*(11), 1595–1619.

Macdonald, S., & Kam, J. (2007). Aardvark et al.: Quality journals and gamesmanship in management studies. *Journal of Information Science and Engineering, 33*(6), 702–717.

MacIntosh, R., Mason, K., Beech, N., & Bartunek, J.M. (2021). *Delivering Impact in Management Research: When Does it Really Happen?* Abingdon: Routledge.

Mackenzie, N., Pittaki, Z., & Wong, N. (2019). Historical approaches for hospitality and tourism research. *International Journal of Contemporary Hospitality Management, 32*(4), 1469–1485.

McLaren, P., Mills, A., & Weatherbee, T. (Eds.). (2015). *The Routledge Companion to Management and Organizational History*. Abingdon: Routledge.

Maclean, M., Harvey, C., & Clegg, S. (2016). Conceptualising historical organization studies. *Academy of Management Review, 41*(4), 609–632.

Maclean, M., Harvey, C., & Clegg, S.R. (2017). Organization theory in business and management history: Present status and future prospects. *Business History Review, 91*(3), 457–481.

Maclean, M., Harvey, C., & Suddaby, R. (2020). Institutional entrepreneurship and the field of power: The emergence of the global hotel industry. In M. Maclean, S.R. Clegg, R. Suddaby, & C. Harvey (Eds.), *Historical Organization Studies: Theory and Applications* (pp. 149–169). London: Routledge.

Maclean, M., Harvey, C., Sillince, J.A.A., & Golant, B.D. (2014). Living up to the past? Ideological sensemaking in organizational transition. *Organization, 21*(4), 543–567.

Maclean, M., Harvey, C., Sillince, J.A.A., & Golant, B.D. (2018). Intertextuality, rhetorical history and the uses of the past in organizational transition. *Organization Studies, 39*(12), 1733–1755.

Maclean, M., Harvey, C., Suddaby, R., & Clegg, S.R. (2020). Advancing new directions for organizational research. In M. Maclean, S.R. Clegg, R. Suddaby, & C. Harvey (Eds.), *Historical Organization Studies: Theory and Applications* (pp. 3–22). London: Routledge.

Markley, G. (2008). The Coca-Cola Company archives: Thriving where dilbert, not Schellenberg, matters. *Provenance, Journal of the Society of Georgia Archivists, 26*(1), 3–23.

Marris, R. (1963). A model of managerial enterprise. *Quarterly Journal of Economics, 77*(2), 185–209.

McCraw. T. (1997). *Creating Modern Capitalism*. Cambridge, MA: Harvard University Press.

McGaughey, S.L. (2013). Institutional entrepreneurship in North American lightning protection standards: Rhetorical history and unintended consequences of failure. *Business History, 55*(1), 73–97.

Mena, S., Rintamäki, J., Fleming, P., & Spicer, A. (2016). On the forgetting of corporate irresponsibility. *Academy of Management Review, 41*(4), 720–738.

Miller, S. (2020). *The Importance of Teaching History in Business Schools*. https://som.yale.edu/blog/the-importance-of-teaching-history-in-business-schools?blog=75818.

Mills, A.J., Suddaby, R., Foster, W., & Durepos, G. (2016). Re-visiting the historic turn 10 years later: Current debates in management and organizational history. *Management & Organizational History, 11*(2), 67–76.

Minefee, I., & Bucheli, M. (2021). MNC responses to international NGO activist campaigns: Evidence from Royal Dutch/Shell in apartheid South Africa. *Journal of International Business Studies, 52*(5), 971–998.

Mintzberg, H. (1996). Managing Government, Governing Management, *Harvard Business Review*, (May–June 1996).

Mooney, P. (1982). Commentary I. *American Archivist, 45*(3), 291–293.

Mooney, P. (1993). The practice of history in Corporate America: Business archives in the United States. In A. Jones & P. Cantelon (Eds.), *Corporate Archives and History: Making the Past Work* (pp. 9–20). Malabar, FL: Kreiger Publishing Company.

Morck, R., & Yeung, B. (2007). History in perspective: Comment on Jones and Khanna 'Bringing history (back) into international business. *Journal of International Business Studies, 38*(2), 357–360.

Muldoon, J. (2019). Stubborn things: Evidence, postmodernism and the craft of history. *Journal of Management History, 25*(1), 125–136.

Muldoon, J. (2020), Methodologies within management history. In Bowden, B., Muldoon, J., Gould, A.M. & McMurray, A. (Eds.), The Palgrave Handbook of Management History. London: Palgrave Macmillan.

Murmann, J.P. (2012). Marrying history and social science in strategy research. In S.J. Kahl, B.S. Silverman, & M.A. Cusumano (Eds.), *Advances in Strategic Management* (pp. 89–115). Bingley: Emerald Group.

Musacchio Adorisio, A.L. (2014). Organizational remembering as narrative: 'Storying' the past in banking. *Organization, 21*(4), 463–476.

Mutch, A. (2020). Writing the history of practices. In M. Maclean, S.R. Clegg, R. Suddaby, & C. Harvey (Eds.), *Historical Organization Studies: Theory and Applications* (pp. 26–38). London: Routledge.

Myrick, K., Helms Mills, J., & Mills, A. (2013) History-making and the Academy of Management: an ANTi-History perspective, *Management & Organizational History, 8*(4), 345–370.

Nissley, N., & Casey, A. (2002). The politics of the exhibition: Viewing corporate museums through the paradigmatic lens of organizational memory. *British Journal of Managment, 13*, 35–45.

Oertel, S., & Thommes, K. (2015). Making history: Sources of organizational history and its rhetorical construction. *Scandinavian Journal of Management, 31*(4), 549–560.

Oertel, S., & Thommes, K. (2018). History as a source of organizational identity creation. *Organization Studies, 39*(12), 1709–1731.

Ooi, C. (2002). Persuasive histories: Decentering, recentering and the emotional crafting of the past. *Journal of Organizational Change Management, 15*(6), 606–621.

Ownership Commission Report (2012). Plurality, Stewardship and Engagement. The Ownership Commission. Ownership-commission-2012.pdf (mutuo.coop).

Pant, A., & Ramachandran, J. (2017). Navigating identity duality in multinational subsidiaries: A paradox lens on identity claims at Hindustan Unilever 1959–2015. *Journal of International Business Studies, 48*(6), 664–692.

Parker, M. (2002). Contesting histories: Unity and division in a building society. *Journal of Organizational Change Management, 15*(6), 589–605.

Pavan, R.J. (1977). *Strutture e Strategie delle Imprese Italiane*. Bologna: Bologna University Press.

Peng, M.W., Ahlstrom, D., Carraher, S.M., & Shi, W. (stone). (2017). An institution-based view of global IPR history. *Journal of International Business Studies, 48*(7), 893–907.

Penrose, E.T. (1995). *The Theory of the Growth of the Firm.* Oxford: Oxford University Press. (Original work published 1959).

Perchard, A., MacKenzie, N.G., Decker, S., & Favero, G. (2017). Clio in the business school: Historical approaches in strategy, international business and entrepreneurship. *Business History, 59*(6), 904–927.

Pettigrew, A. (1985). *The Awakening Giant: Continuity and Change in Imperial Chemical Industries.* Abingdon: Routledge.

Pettigrew, A., Thomas, H., & Whittington, R. (2002). The strengths and limitations of a field. In A. Pettigrew, H. Thomas, & R. Whittington (Eds.), *Handbook of Strategy and Management* (pp. 3–30). London: Sage Publications.

Petty, R.E., & Cacioppo, J.T. (1986). *Communication and Persuasion: Central and Peripheral Routes to Attitude Change.* New York: Springer-Verlag.

Pfeffer, J., & Fong, C.T. (2002). The end of business schools? Less success than meets the eye. *Academy of Management Learning & Education, 1*(1), 78–95.

Phillips, N. (2019). What is academic success anyway? A rejoinder to 'confronting' the crisis of confidence in management studies. *Academy of Management Learning and Education, 18*(2), 306–309.

Phillips, R., Schrempf-Stirling, J., & Stutz, C. (2020). The past, history, and corporate social responsibility. *Journal of Business Ethics: JBE, 166*(2), 203–213.

Pillai, Sandeep D., Goldfarb, B., & Kirsch, David A. (2020). The origins of firm strategy: Learning by economic experimentation and strategic pivots in the early automobile industry. *Strategic Management Journal, 41*(3), 369–399.

Pino, F. (2012). After the mergers wave: Change management and the building of the Intesa Sanpaolo Group Archives. In Shibusawa Eiichi Memorial Foundation (Ed.), *Leveraging Corporate Assets: New Global Directions for Business Archives* (pp. 87–94). Tokyo: Shibusawa Eiichi Memorial Foundation.

Piore, M., & Sabel, C. (1984). *The Second Industrial Divide: Possibilities for Prosperity.* London: Basic Books.

Poor, S., Novicevic, M.M., Humphreys, J.H., & Popoola, I.T. (2016). Making history happen: A genealogical analysis of Colt's rhetorical history. *Management & Organizational History, 11*(2), 147–165.

Popp, A., & Holt, R. (2013). The presence of entrepreneurial opportunity. *Business History, 55*(1), 9–28.

Popp, A., & Fellman, S. (2016). Writing business history: Creating narratives. *Business History, 59*(8), 1242–1260.

Popp, A., & Fellman, S. (2020). Power, archives and the making of rhetorical organizational histories: A stakeholder perspective. *Organization Studies, 41*(11), 1531–1549.

Popp, A., & Wilson, J.F. (2007). Life-cycles, contingency and agency: Growth, development and decline in English industrial districts and clusters. *Environment & Planning A, 39*, 2975–2992.

Porter, M. (1990). *The Competitive Advantage of Nations*. Boston, MA: Harvard University Press.

Prechel, H. (2000). *Big Business and the State: Historical Transitions and Corporate Transformations, 1880s–1990s*. New York: SUNY Press.

Quail, J. (2000). The proprietorial theory of the firm. *Journal of Industrial History, 3*(1), reprinted in J.F. Wilson, N.D Wong, & S. Toms (Eds.), *Management and Industry. Case Studies in UK Industrial History* (pp. 73–110). Abingdon: Routledge, .

Rabchuk, G. (1997). Life after the 'Big Bang': Business archives in an era of disorder. *The American Archivist, 60*(1), 34–43.

Reader, W.J. (1970). *Imperial Chemical Industries: A History*, Vol. 1. Oxford: Oxford University Press.

Rose, M.B. (1993). Beyond Buddenbrooks: The family firm and the management of succession in nineteenth century Britain. In J. Brown & M. B. Rose (Eds.), *Entrepreneurship, Networks and Modern Business* (pp. 130–152). Manchester: Manchester University Press.

Rowlinson, M., & Procter, S. (1999). Organizational culture and business history. *Organization Studies, 20*(3), 369–396.

Rowlinson, M., & Delahaye, A. (2009). The cultural turn in business history. *Enterprise et Histoire, 55*, 90–110.

Rowlinson, M., & Hassard, J. (1993). The invention of corporate culture: A history of the histories of Cadbury. *Human Relations; Thousand Oaks, 46*(3), 299–326.

Rowlinson, M., Hassard, J., & Decker, S. (2014). Research strategies for organizational history: A dialogue between historical theory and organization theory. *Academy of Management Review. Academy of Management, 39*(3), 250–274.

Rowlinson, M., Toms, S., & Wilson, J.F. (2007). Competing perspectives on the 'managerial revolution': From 'managerialist' to 'anti-managerialist'. *Business History, 49*(4), 464–482.

Roy, W.G. (1999). *Socialising Capital: The Rise of the Large Industrial Corporation in America*. Princeton, NJ: Princeton University Press.

Ruef, Martin. (2020). The household as a source of labor for entrepreneurs: Evidence from New York City during industrialization. *Strategic Entrepreneurship Journal, 14*(1), 20–42.

Russell, A., & Vinsel, L. (2018). After innovation, turn to maintenance. *Technology and Culture 59*, 1–25.

Sabel, C., & Zeitlin, J. (1985). Historical alternatives to mass production: Politics, markets and technology in nineteenth century industrialization. *Past and Present, 108*, 152–180.

Sakai, K. (2020). Institutional change as historical confluence: The development of the nursing profession in Japan. In M. Maclean, S.R. Clegg, R.

Suddaby, & C. Harvey (Eds.), *Historical Organization Studies: Theory and Applications* (pp. 188–206). London: Routledge.

Sandhu, S., Perera, S., & Sardeshmunk, S. (2019). Chartered courses and meandering trails: Crafting success and impact as business school academics. *Academy of Management Learning and Education, 18*(2), 153–185.

Sasaki, I., Ravasi, D., Kotlar, J., & Vaara, E. (2019). Dealing with revered past: Historical identity statements and strategic change in Japanese family firms. *Strategic Management Journal, 41*(3), 590–623.

Schrempf-Stirling, J., Palazzo, G., & Phillips, R.A. (2016). Historic corporate social responsibility. *Academy of Management Review, 41*(4), 700–719.

Schultz, M., & Hernes, T. (2013). A temporal perspective on organizational identity. *Organization Science, 24*(1), 1–21.

Schumpeter, J.A. (1947). The creative response in economic history. *Journal of Economic History, 7*(2), 149–159.

Schumpeter, J.A. (1949). Economic theory and entrepreneurial history. In R.R. Wohl (Ed.), *Change and the Entrepreneur: Postulates and Patterns for Entrepreneurial History* (pp. 63–84). Cambridge, MA: Harvard University Press.

Scranton, P. (1983). *Proprietary Capitalism: The Textile Manufacture at Philadelphia.* New York: Cambridge University Press.

Scranton, P. (1989). *Figured Tapestry: Production, Markets and Power in Philadelphia Textiles, 1855–1941.* New York: Cambridge University Press.

Scranton, P. (1991). A review of *Scale and Scope. Technology and Culture, 32*(4), 385–393.

Scranton, P. (1997). *Endless Novelty: Speciality Production and American Industrialization, 1865–1925.* Princeton, NJ: Princeton University Press.

Scranton, P., & Fridenson, P. (2013). *Reimagining Business History.* Baltimore, MD: John Hopkins University Press.

Scranton, P. (2019). Fixing holes in the plan: Maintenance and repair in Poland, 1945–1970. *Enterprise et Histoire, 103*, 54–72.

Scranton, P. (2020). Collaboration, coordination, cooperation and subversive entrepreneurship in Socialist Hungary', paper given to the Business History Conference.

Sharma, G., & Bansal, P. (2020). Cocreating rigorous and relevant knowledge. *Academy of Management Journal, 63*(2), 386–410.

Shenkar, O. (2021). Using interdisciplinary lenses to enrich the treatment of culture in international business. *International Business Review, 30*(2), 101799.

Smith, A., & Johns, J. (2020). Historicizing modern slavery: Free-grown sugar as an ethics-driven market category in nineteenth-century Britain. *Journal of Business Ethics: JBE, 166*(2), 271–292.

Smith, A., & Simeone, D. (2017). Learning to use the past: The development of a rhetorical history strategy by the London headquarters of the Hudson's Bay Company. *Management & Organizational History, 12*(4), 334–356.

Smith, G. (2007). Management history and historical context: Potential benefits of its inclusion in the management curriculum. *Academy of Management Learning & Education, 6*(4), 522–533.

Starkey, K., & Madan, P. (2001). Bridging the relevance gap: Aligning stakeholders in the future of management research. *British Journal of Management, 12*(s1), S3–S26.

Stinchcombe, A.L. (1965). Social structure and organizations. In J.G. March (Ed.), *Handbook of Organizations* (Vol. 7, pp. 142–193). Chicago, IL: Rand McNally.

Stutz, C., & Schrempf-Stirling, J. (2019). Using the past responsibly: What responsible managers and management academics can learn from historians' professional ethics. In O. Laasch, D. Jamali, R.E. Freeman, & R. Suddaby. (Eds.), *Research Handbook of Responsible Management* (pp. 742–755). London: Edward Elgar.

Suddaby, R. (2010). Challenges for institutional theory. *Journal of Management Enquiry, 19*(1), 14–20.

Suddaby, R. (2016). Toward a historical consciousness: Following the historic turn in management thought. *M@N@Gement, 19*(1), 46–60.

Suddaby, R., & Foster, W.M. (2017). History and organizational change. *Journal of Management, 43*(1), 19–38.

Suddaby, R., & Greenwood, R. (2005). Rhetorical strategies of legitimacy. *Administrative Science Quarterly, 50*(1), 35–67.

Suddaby, R., Foster, W.M., & Quinn Trank, C. (2010). Rhetorical history as a source of competitive advantage. In B.J.A.C., & L. Joseph (Eds.), *The Globalization of Strategy Research* (*Advances in Strategic Management*, Vol. 27, pp. 147–173). Bingley: Emerald Group Publishing Limited.

Suddaby, R., Coraiola, D., Harvey, C., & Foster, W (2020). History and the micro-foundations of dynamic capabilities. *Strategic Management Journal, 41*(3), 530–556.

Taylor, S., Bell, E., & Cooke, B. (2009). Business history and the historiographical operation. *Management & Organizational History, 4*(2), 151–166.

Teece, D.J. (1993). The dynamics of industrial capitalism: Perspectives on Alfred Chandler's scale and scope. *Journal of Economic Literature, 31*(1), 199–225.

Teece, D.J. (2011). Achieving integration of the business school curriculum using the dynamic capabilities framework. *The Journal of Management Development, 30*(5), 499–518.

Teece, D.J., Pisano, G., & Shuen, A. (1997). Dynamic capabilities and strategic management. *Strategic Management Journal, 18*(7), 509–533.

Tennent, K.D, Gillett, A.G., & Foster, W.M. (2019). Developing historical consciousness in management learners. *Management Learning, 51*(1), 73–88.

Thompson, N. (2018). Hey DJ, don't stop the music: Institutional work and record pooling practices in the United States' music industry. *Business History, 60*(5), 677–698.

Tilba, A. (2017). Evolution of UK corporate ownership and control: Governance, complexity and context. In J.F. Wilson, S. Toms, A. de Jong, & E.

Buchnea (Eds.), *The Routledge Companion to Business History* (pp. 300–316). Abington, Oxon: Routledge.

Tilba, A., & Wilson, J.F. (2017). Vocabularies of motive and temporal perspectives: Examples of pension fund engagement and disengagement. *British Journal of Management, 28*(3), 502–518.

Toms, S., & Wright, M. (2002). Corporate governance, strategy and structure in British business history, 1950–2000. *Business History, 44*, (3), 91–124.

Toms, S., & Wilson, J.F. (2003). Scale, scope and accountability: Towards a new paradigm in British business history. *Business History, 45*(4), 1–23.

Toms, S., & Wright, M. (2005a). Corporate governance, strategy and refocusing: US and British comparatives, 1950–2000'. *Business History, 47*, 267–295.

Toms, S., & Wright, M. (2005b). Divergence and Convergence within Anglo-American Corporate Governance Systems: Evidence from the US and UK, 1950–2000. *Business History, 47*(2), 267–295.

Toms, S. (2010). Value, profit and risk: Accounting and the resource-based view of the firm. *Accounting, Auditing & Accountability Journal, 23*(5), 647–670.

Toms, S., & Fleischman, R.K. (2015). Accounting fundamentals and accounting change: Boulton & Watt and the Springfield Armory. *Accounting, Organizations and Society, 41*, 1–20i.

Toms, S., & Wilson, J. (2010). In defence of business history: A reply to Taylor, Bell and Cooke. *Management & Organizational History, 5*(1), 109–120.

Toms, S., & Wilson, J. (2012). Revisiting Chandler on the theory of the firm. In M. Dietrich & J. Kraft (Eds.), *Handbook on the Economics and Theory of the Firm*. Cheltenham: Edward Elgar, pp. 280–295.

Toms, S., Wilson, N., & Wright, M. (2015). The evolution of private equity: Corporate restructuring in the UK, c. 1945–2010. *Business History, 57*(5), 736–768.

Toms, S., & Wilson, J.F. (2017). Business history: Agendas, historiography and debates. In J. Wilson, S. Toms, A. de Jong, & E. Buchnea (Eds.), *The Routledge Companion to Business History* (pp. 9–18). Abingdon: Routledge.

Toms, S. (2018). Financial scandals: A historical overview. *Accounting and Business Research, 49*(5), 477–499.

Toms, S., Wilson, N., & Wright, M. (2020). Innovation, intermediation, and the nature of entrepreneurship: A historical perspective. *Strategic Entrepreneurship Journal, 14*(1), 105–121.

Transparency Taskforce (TTF). (2020). How can we accelerate the rebuilding of trust and confidence in financial services? *White Paper* https://www.transparencytaskforce.org/app/download/5814071764/TTF+WHITE+PAPER+V5+DIGITAL.pdf

Usdiken, B., & Kipping, M. (2014). History and organization studies: A long-term view. In M. Bucheli & R.D. Wadhwani (Eds.), *Organizations in Time: History, Theory, Methods* (pp. 33–55). Oxford: Oxford University Press.

Vaara, E., & Lamberg, J. A. (2016). Taking historical embeddedness seriously: Three historical approaches to advance strategy process and practice research. *Academy of Management Review, 41*(4), 633–657.

Vacca, F. (2014). Knowledge in memory: Corporate and museum archives. *Fashion Practice, 6*(2), 273–288.

Van Aken, J.E. (2004). Management research based on the paradigm of the design science: The quest for field tested and grounded technological rules. *Journal of Management Studies, 41*(2), 219–246.

Van de Ven, A.H. (2007). *Engaged Scholarship: A Guide for Organizational and Social Research*. New York: Oxford University Press.

Van de Ven, A.H., & Johnson, P.E. (2006). Knowledge for theory and practice. *Academy of Management Review, 31*, 802–821.

Van Fleet, D.D., & Wren, D.A. (2005). Teaching history in business schools: 1982–2003. *Academy of Management Learning and Education, 4*(1), 44–56.

Van Lent, W., & Smith, A.D. (2019). Perceiving the present by means of the past: Theorizing the strategic importance of corporate archives. In T.J. Andersen, T. Simon, & L. Stefan (Eds.), *Strategic Responsiveness and Adaptive Organizations: New Research Frontiers in International Strategic Management* (pp. 97–110). Bingley: Emerald Publishing Limited.

Van Lent, W., & Durepos, G. (2019a). Nurturing the historic turn: "history as theory" versus "history as method". *Journal of Management History, 25*(4), 429–443.

Van Lent, W., & Smith, A.D. (2020). Using versus excusing: The Hudson's Bay Company's long-term engagement with its (problematic) past. *Journal of Business Ethics: JBE, 166*(2), 215–231.

Verbeke, A., & Kano, L. (2015). The new internalization theory and multinational enterprises from emerging economies: A business history perspective. *Business History Review, 89*(3), 415–445.

Voronov, M., De Clercq, D., & Hinings, C.R. (2013). Conformity and distinctiveness in a global institutional framework: The legitimation of Ontario fine wine. *Journal of Management Studies, 50*(4), 607–645.

Wadhwani, D., & Jones, G. (2016). Historical change and the competitive advantage of firms: Explicating the "dynamics" in the dynamic capabilities framework. Harvard Business School Working Paper, 17–052.

Wadhwani, R. Daniel, & Lubinski, C. (2017). Reinventing entrepreneurial history. *Business History Review, 91*(4), 767–799.

Wadhwani, R.D., Suddaby, R., Mordhorst, M., & Popp, A. (2018). History as organizing: Uses of the past in organization studies. *Organization Studies, 39*(12), 1663–1683.

Wadhwani, R. Daniel, Kirsch, D., Welter, F., Gartner, William B., & Jones, G. G. (2020). Context, time, and change: Historical approaches to entrepreneurship research. *Strategic Entrepreneurship Journal, 14*(1), 3–19.

Warren, R., & Tweedale, G. (2002). Business ethics and business history: Neglected dimensions in management education. *British Journal of Management, 13*(3), 209–219.

Webster, T. (2019). Co-operation and globalisation: The British co-operative wholesales, the co-operative group and the world since 1863. London: Routledge. ISBN 9781138501355

Webster, T., Shaw L., & Vorberg-Rugh R. (2016b). Introduction. In Tony Webster, L. Shaw, & R. Vorberg-Rugh (Eds.), *Mainstreaming Co-operation: An Alternative for the Twenty-first Century?* (pp. 1–13). Manchester: Manchester University Press, 2016.* ISBN 9781526100993

Webster, T., Shaw, L., Vorberg-Rugh, R., Wilson, J.F., & Snaith, I. (2016a). Learning to swim against the tide: Crises and co-operative credibility – some international and historical examples. In Tony Webster, L. Shaw, & R. Vorberg-Rugh (Eds.), *Mainstreaming Co-operation: An Alternative for the Twenty-first Century?* (pp. 280–304). Manchester: Manchester University Press. ISBN 9781526100993

Webster, T., Wilson, J.F., & Vorberg-Rugh, R. (2017). Going global. The rise of the CWS as an international commercial and political actor, 1863–1950: Scoping an agenda for further research. In M. Hilson, S. Neunsinger, & G. Patmore (Eds.), *A Global History of Consumer Co-operation since 1850: Movements and Businesses, 28, Studies in Global Social History* (pp. 559–583). Leiden: Brill. ISBN 9789004336544

Webster, T., Wilson, J., & Wong, N. (2020). Commerce with a bit of ethics or ethics with a bit of commerce? The conundrum of British consumer co-operation 1863–1990. *Journal of Management History.* doi.org/10.1108/jmh-01-2020-0008

Welch, C., & Piekkari, R. (2017). How should we (not) judge the 'quality'of qualitative research? A re-assessment of current evaluative criteria in International Business. *Journal of World Business, 52*(5), 714–725.

Whittington, R., & Mayer, M. (2000). *The European Corporation: Strategy, Structure and Social Science.* Oxford: Oxford University Press.

Whittington, R. (2008). Alfred Chandler, founder of strategy: Lost tradition and renewed inspiration. *Business History Review, 82*(2), 267–277.

Whittle, A., & Wilson, J.F. (2015). Ethnomethodology and the production of history: Studying 'history-in-action'. *Business History, 57*(1), 41–63.

Wilkins, M. (1970). *The Emergence of Multinational Enterprise.* Boston, MA: Harvard University Press.

Wilkins, M. (1974), *The Maturing of Multinational Enterprise.* Boston, MA: Harvard University Press.

Wilkins, M. (1988). The free-standing company, 1870–1914: An important type of British foreign direct investment. *Economic History Review, 41*(2), 259–282.

Williamson, O.E. (1985). *The Economic Institutions of Capitalism.* New York: Simon and Schuster.

Wilson, C. (1954). *The History of Unilever, A Study in Economic Growth and Social.* London: Cassell and Company.

Wilson, J.F. (1995). *British Business History, 1720–1994.* Manchester: Manchester University Press.

Wilson, J.F. (1996). Management education in Britain: A compromise between culture and necessity. In R.P. Amdam (Ed.), *Management, Education and Competitiveness: Europe, Japan and the United States* (pp. 133–149). Abingdon: Routledge.

Wilson, J.F. (1998). `International business strategies at Ferranti, 1907–1975: Direction, management and performance. *Business History,40*(1), 100–121.

Wilson, J.F., & Popp, A. (Eds.). (2003). *Industrial Clusters and Regional Business Networks in England, 1750–1970.* Farnham: Ashgate.

Wilson, J.F., & Thomson, A. (2006). *The Making of Modern Management: British Management in Historical Perspective.* Oxford: Oxford University Press.

Wilson, J.F., & Thomson, A. (2007). Management in historical perspective: stages and paradigms. *Competition and Change, 10*(4), 357–374.

Wilson, J.F., Webster, A., & Vorberg-Rugh, R. (2013). *Building Co-operation. A History of The Co-operative Group, 1863–2013.* Oxford: Oxford University Press.

Wilson, J.F. (2014). Future of British co-operatives rests on radical new thinking. *The Huffington Post,* https://www.huffingtonpost.co.uk/professor-john-wilson/british-cooperatives_b_5190045.html

Wilson, J., Toms, S., de Jong, A., & Buchnea, E. (2016). *The Routledge Companion to Business History.* Abingdon: Routledge.

Wilson, J.F., Buchnea, E., & Tilba, A. (2018). The British corporate network, 1904–1976: Revisiting the finance–industry relationship. *Business History,* 60(1), 1–28.

Wright, R. (2010). Teaching history in business schools: An insider's view. *Academy of Management Learning and Education, 9*(4), 697–700.

Yacob, S. (2009). Hidden disciplines in Malaysia: The role of business history in a multi-disciplinary framework. *Australian Economic History Review, 49*(3), 302–324.

Yates, J. (2014). Understanding historical methods in organization studies. In M. Bucheli & R.D. Wadhwani (Eds.), *Organizations in Time: History, Theory and Methods.* (pp. 265–283). Oxford: Oxford University Press.

Ybema, S. (2014). The invention of transitions: History as a symbolic site for discursive struggles over organizational change. *Organization, 21*(4), 495–513.

Zald, M.N. (1993). Organization studies as a scientific and humanistic enterprise: Toward a reconceptualization of the foundations of the field. *Organization Science, 4*(4), 513–528.

Index

Note: *Italic* page numbers refer to figures.

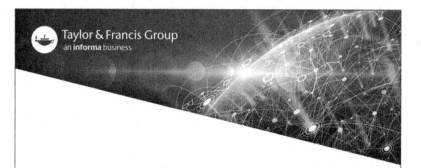

Printed in the United States
by Baker & Taylor Publisher Services